Creative Sampler Embroidery

Creative Sampler Embroidery

Caroline Vincent

The Crowood Press

First published in 2002 by
The Crowood Press Ltd
Ramsbury, Marlborough
Wiltshire SN8 2HR

www.crowood.com

British Library Cataloguing-in-Publication Data
A catalogue record for this book is available from the
British Library.

ISBN 1 86126 528 X

Acknowledgements

I am grateful to Cara Ackerman of DMC Creative
World for so generously supplying the Zweigart
fabrics and DMC Threads; Sally Jefferson of Coats
Craft UK for every assistance in supplying Anchor
Threads; Colin Fulford of Fulford Software
Solutions for offering advice and guidance; and
my family Ted, Peter and Johnnie for their help
and support.

In order to further illustrate some of my techniques
and ideas, I have used details from several of my
commissioned pieces and I would like to thank
everyone concerned for so kindly agreeing to the
loan of the work: Ms Gina Banns, Mr and Mrs
Simon Green and family, Angela and Richard
Saffery, Mrs Janet Saunders and Hollie Saunders,
Mr and Mrs Simon Wood and family.

Typefaces used: Giovanni (main text and headings);
Tiepolo (chapter titles).

Typeset and designed by
D & N Publishing
Baydon, Marlborough, Wiltshire.

Printed and bound in Malaysia by Times Offset (M) Sdn.
Bhd.

Contents

1 Introduction

Over the years I have received many comments about my embroideries, with repeated requests for patterns and information on the techniques I use to create the particular textural effects. I have therefore put together a series of projects that include a number of elements from my own designs, whilst at the same time using the opportunity to develop and explore several new ideas and approaches. Each project is based on a theme, and I have planned the compositions so as to incorporate as wide a range of motifs as possible, without making any one design too complicated or involved. Cross-stitch has always been the favourite technique for sampler embroidery, and this simple and versatile stitch goes to make up the majority of the designs, as its intrinsic squared form gives the motifs their singular stylized character. However, samplers originally included a variety of other techniques and it was the different characteristics and functions of the individual stitches that gave the embroideries their rich textural qualities. Working a large design purely in one style of stitch can be very tedious, and also the end results may be rather disappointing, whereas the inclusion of a few other stitch techniques, or even slight variations on the construction of one particular stitch, will create a more visually exciting and interesting piece of work.

However, I have found that it is not always the type of stitch that requires consideration, when trying to depict a particular subject, and quite often it is the choice of colour that needs to be altered in some way. A motif can be completely transformed, by introducing a more varied and subtle range of colours, and the basic structure of a cross-stitch makes this an ideal technique for mixing and blending colours to create a wide range of different effects. For example, the wonderful patterns and texture of stone-flint buildings are achieved simply by combining a group of colours with different tonal values, and likewise many bright and vivid shades can be softened or subdued by the addition of a dull or neutral colour. Nearly every motif in the book has been given an individual set of colours, with the amount of threads used in each combination indicated in the brackets next to the colour codes. The advantage of being able to alter and adjust the intensity and tone of each colour, so as to create an overall harmony between them, brings a sense of unity to the whole design. This method of mixing the shades of thread to make an original colour scheme is now second nature to me, and I hope that you will find it equally exciting and rewarding. I feel that one of the essential qualities that typifies a sampler embroidery is the use of the repeat pattern and I have included decorative elements that suggest the idea of pattern throughout the projects. All the main designs are based on the style of a strip sampler, where the horizontal panels of motifs are divided by narrow bands of repeat patterns. Also, a number of the smaller motifs have been arranged into rows of two or three images of the same design, forming a repeat pattern in themselves, and only relying on the various combinations in colours and textures to differentiate them. In this way a row of hens or a line of sheep have a basic theme that connects them, even though their individual appearance is very different; you might find it fun to make use of this idea in your own designs.

I have planned the five larger projects around a set format, so that although the main outer borders are all different in style and size, the actual width of the main panels is the same in each design. In this way it is quite easy to exchange one panel with another, and to vary the compositions in the projects to suit your own particular theme. Similarly, as all the individual motifs work independently of one another, it is possible to organize your own sampler designs from a selection of the subjects illustrated.

The fabrics I have suggested for the projects are either Aida or Evenweave, and I have stitched the designs using both types of cloth, so that the reader can see that there is no differentiation between the complexity of the work and the type of cloth used. Many embroiderers prefer to work on Aida, as they find it easier to see the holes in the fabric, but quite often I have heard the comment that it is considered an amateur's choice of fabric, and therefore only suitable for easy designs. I had never worked on Aida until I began these projects, and I was absolutely

OPPOSITE: *Embroideries depicting the family home and related subjects are becoming increasingly popular and I made this sampler for my eldest son when he was five years old, as a way of recording his everyday environment at that time. I planned to feature our small cottage together with the many animals that regularly visited the garden, using a combination of stylized patterns and more naturalistic motifs to illustrate the woods, fields and vast pond that represented the surrounding area.*

·19· PETER EDWARD VINCENT ·88·
BURTON COMMON, PETWORTH.

delighted with the results and felt even more convinced that it is probably more to do with the choice of colours, for the cloth and threads, that have earned this fabric its much maligned reputation. I have seen so many embroiderers working with hard primary colours onto a stark white cloth, which emphasizes the obviousness of the holes, whereas a combination of more muted shades will focus the attention on the embroidery motifs and allow the fabric to integrate with the design. I have listed the design sizes and suggested colours for both Aida and Evenweave in the material guide for each project, but the designs are equally suited to any other type of fabric you feel comfortable with.

The finished embroideries may have the appearance of looking quite intricate and complex, but this is only the impression created by an imaginative use of colour and the addition of a few other simple stitches. The majority of prospective sampler makers will be familiar with such basic stitches as back-stitch, satin-stitch and French-knots and as with cross-stitch, once you have made the first stitch there is nothing more to learn. Many of the textural surfaces used to illustrate the motifs rely on a more individual and creative approach, and are not so much about making accurate stitches as about making an individual interpretation. An area of texture, such as the meadow grass or the trees in the country house project, are really quite easy to build up, but if you prefer to work entirely in cross-stitch, I have given alternative colour suggestions alongside the motifs. However, do have a go at some of these ideas, even if it is just practising on some spare fabric to start with. Also there is really nothing more complicated about embarking on a large rather than a smaller project, other than the amount of time you will need to invest. Whatever your level of ability, I hope that the step-by-step diagrams and details will encourage you to approach the projects with confidence, and also act as a springboard for more experienced embroiderers to extend their creative skills.

Colour

I find the whole subject of colour totally fascinating and can spend more time agonizing about the right colour combinations than on any other area of the design. I am always trying out small samples of different colour schemes on spare pieces of fabric, so as to give myself as wide a range of options as possible before committing myself to the actual embroidery. However, even when I feel sure that I have made the right decision, I will often change the colour of a motif, once it is in place, simply by overstitching in another shade. The problem being that as each new colour is added, the whole balance of the existing colours is slightly altered, so that sometimes one area might need either a softer or brighter shade, whereas another motif might require a completely different

colour altogether. Unless it is essential that you unpick the work and begin again, I usually find that I can make enough adjustments simply by reworking the area in another colour.

In the main, the range of colours I usually work with are the more subdued and muted shades, highlighted with the use of brighter, bolder colours in small areas. On a shade card my choice of colours can look positively dull and 'dirty' compared to some of the more vivid, acid hues; but in fact, when they are placed together on the fabric, they instantly come to life and harmonize with each other perfectly. The actual colour choice of the fabric also plays an important part in the overall appearance of the finished design, and needs to be considered in relation to the theme of the embroidery. I am very fond of using off-white and cream threads in my work, and these colours look far more effective when laid on an ecru shade of fabric, which will complement and accentuate their qualities. On the other hand, I find the two most difficult colours to work with are pure white and black, and only use these colours when necessary to the design, and more usually just in small areas for highlighting, or to accentuate detail.

The colour schemes I have suggested for the following projects have been carefully worked out using many tried and tested combinations; but obviously in the end they are essentially my own personal choice, and you are quite welcome to alter and substitute colours where ever you wish. Although a selection of coloured skeins can look very attractive and enticing when placed together as a group, the very same colours have a tendency to appear rather flat and monotonous when embroidered as cross-stitch over large areas. In order to avoid this rather bland effect, I have developed the techniques of mixing and blending threads and overstitching areas of cross-stitch to create more light and shade in the composition and give more depth to the colours.

Simply by working with three strands of different colours, it is possible to create a wide variety of effects, through the twisting and blending of the threads as they are stitched. This technique has proved to be an excellent way of interpreting the textural surfaces of buildings, as it gives a more realistic appearance to materials such as flint, brick, stone, tiles and gravel. To achieve these results it is necessary to choose shades of light, medium and dark tones, and also for the colours themselves to be very different from each other, or they will tend to merge together to make one colour. For example, a roof might work well by combining a neutral grey with a medium green and a deep rust red, which would give the feeling of light and shade as well as a colour variation, even when worked in cross-stitch.

Another method of using colour to create more depth and richness in a piece of work, is by overstitching one area of colour in an alternative shade of thread with a different tonal value. Usually the darker colours are best used to cover the base of the motif and then lighter shades are applied in such a way as to allow the base colours to show through, making an exciting combination of colours and texture. This technique is ideal for interpreting natural elements such as grass and water, where a cross-stitch area can be worked first, and then overstitched using a long straight-stitch, in another range of colours.

Although the basic group of colours you first select for a project may be quite limited, you will find that the above mentioned techniques, of mixing and blending, will necessitate the inclusion of small amounts of a number of other colours. As long as all the colours work in harmony together, and you use the main colours throughout the design, the only drawback will be the added expense of buying extra shades. However, once you have built up a collection of colours you are familiar with, you will find that you re-use them repeatedly in future projects; as an example I have listed a range of the colours that I use as the basis for all my designs. I have also found it helpful to decide on a basic colour theme to any new design, and whether it will have an overall feeling of being warm or cool as this will make it easier to select complementary colour combinations. For example, if you had designed a decorative border of flowers and chose a bluish pink such as DMC 316, the leaves would probably work more successfully in a green such as DMC 502, which also has a bluish tint. Whereas a pink such as DMC 224 would match well with the green DMC 522, both colours having a more reddish tint.

Another significant clue in making colour choices is to consider the type of occasion the embroidery is intended to commemorate. Whether it is to celebrate a birth, marriage, anniversary, record the family home, or simply as a gift for a particular person, all these factors will influence the decisions you need to make in order to achieve the desired effect in the embroidery. For instance, should it be lively, serene, or sophisticated in style; and also whether it be decorative or formal.

In fact, there is actually no absolute right or wrong where colours are concerned. The decisions you make are a very personal choice and can be influenced as much by your emotions, as the quality of light at the time you make them. This can all sound quite complicated but I have listed a few suggestions, to help make it easier for you to select a suitable colour scheme for your own designs.

Points to Remember When Choosing Colours

◆ Refer to the subject you are working from and select a basic range of colours that will best illustrate its potential, at the same time bearing mind the colour of the fabric you will use.
◆ Remember that the embroidery is always your interpretation of a subject, and that some colours, which might initially seem to be the right choice for a particular motif, may need to be adapted to work with the colour adjacent to it.

◆ Begin with a basic palette of about ten colours, keeping in mind their overall tendency to blue or red shades.
◆ Try to use these basic colours throughout the work, so that colours used on motifs in the centre of the design will also be included within the borders.
◆ Take care that you select the colours in a good light, and never make decisions by electric light during the evening.
◆ Colours can easily take on a different aspect once they are placed next to each other as the embroidery builds up, and remember it is always possible to rework a colour that looks out of place.

Colour Palette

I have found that over the years I have put together a group of colours that I use repeatedly in my work. I have now become so familiar with their intrinsic qualities, that I am often able to immediately visualize their possibilities when I am trying to make a particular colour combination. I have used this basic palette of colours throughout the book, interspersed with the addition of small amounts of several different colours, depending on the various themes of the projects. Although the list of colours for some of the projects might seem rather long, once you have built up a collection of these base colours you will find that you use them time and again. I have indicated the colours that are required as a full skein in each project, and this is usually for the borders, when it is advisable to make sure you have enough from the outset, as occasionally there are small variations between the dye lots.

Beige to Brown

DMC 613, 612, 611, 610 AND ANCHOR 391, 392, 393
This group of neutral colours is probably the most widely used in my designs, and is included, in one way or another, in nearly every piece of work. I find these colours absolutely essential: not only as colours in their own right, but because they seem to have the ability to blend and mix so perfectly with other shades. A single thread of DMC 612 or 611, combined with a red or blue for instance, will create a subtle earthy shade, and make it possible to use quite vivid colours without their appearing too brash and startling. Similarly, I find that the addition of DMC 613, to what I call my 'white' threads, will also help to give a more varied and denser hue. I have used just such a combination in the wide floral border at the top of the country house project where these two examples are illustrated perfectly.

DMC 434 AND 801

These two rich brown colours are from the same group on the colour chart, and I find them the most versatile of the deep-brown spectrum. DMC 434, in particular, seems to have a facility to adapt itself to fit in with any colour scheme, and adds depth and interest when blended with cooler colours.

DMC 3371 AND ANCHOR 905

I often use one or other of these two browns to suggest a black colour, as they are both dark enough to take on the appearance of a sooty-black. When worked as a line of back-stitch using a single thread, either of them is very useful as a means of separating one area of colour from another; for instance, when defining the edge of a roof from the walls of a building.

Yellows

DMC 783, 782, 680, 729, 676, 725

On the colour chart, DMC 783 and 782 look rather dark and dull, and yet whenever I place them on the ecru fabrics they positively sing out. I use these two colours regularly as my bright yellows, and only need to add DMC 725 in small amounts when I need to accentuate a particular detail. DMC 680, 729 and 676 are another family of yellows, and I always refer to them as my straw colours, as they illustrate that subject so well. A wonderful warm gold tone can be made using DMC 729, either on its own or blended with one of the colours listed above, which can make an excellent option for the narrow borders I use to divide the text and motifs.

White and Cream

DMC 746, 3823 AND ANCHOR 386

I have never actually used a real white in any of my work, as I find it such a harsh, cold colour and it tends to eclipse every colour around it. My brightest 'white' is DMC 746, which is in fact a cream, but once it is placed on the ecru fabrics it takes on the appearance of a beautiful soft white. Another problem with light colours is that the slight shadows caused by the cross-stitch make the squareness of the actual stitch very pronounced. One way of disguising this is by including one or even two threads of a pale beige tone, such

OPPOSITE: This second family portrait was made for my youngest son and is also dated the year I finished it. In contrast to the woodland animals that inhabited the common, I decided to give this embroidery a farming theme, and include a range of very different motifs. I also wanted to feature a completely different style of building and, as we lived next to Mill Farm, I thought for a while about using a barn. However, I then realized that the old mill building would make the perfect subject, especially as the children had spent so much time playing down by the stream.

as DMC 613 or Anchor 391. This will create a subtle random pattern as the threads twist together in the embroidery, and distract the eye from the uniformity of the stitch.

On first impressions, DMC 3823 and Anchor 386 may appear very similar, as they are both in the yellow spectrum, but in fact the former has a slightly deeper tinge, which I feel could make quite a difference over a large area. I use these colours constantly as my cream/whites and find that the warm tones perfectly complement any surrounding colours of a deeper hue.

Black and Grey

DMC 310 AND ANCHOR 401

Although we may know that something is black in colour, it can be quite difficult to capture the essence of blackness in a motif. When you view an object of that colour, its surface is in fact always reflecting light, so that what we are actually seeing is something much lighter. If you then simply used the black threads straight from the skein, you would end up with a very dense area of colour that would seem completely lifeless. To help create a more realistic interpretation, you will need to mix the black threads with another, paler colour such as a grey, Anchor 401, or dark brown, Anchor 905. This combination of darker shades will break up the surface area, and give a feeling of life and movement to the subject. The black and white cows in the Meadow Farm project illustrate this point perfectly.

I always use black very sparingly, but occasionally it may be necessary to use it on its own, for example, to define an animal's eye or to separate two colours with a line of back-stitch.

Pink and Red

DMC 316, 3726, 407 AND ANCHOR 13

As one of the basic elements in a sampler is a decorative border of flowers, it is a good idea to build up a range of pinks that will work well with a number of other colours. My favourite shades, which I have used repeatedly throughout the projects, mainly come from the blue-end of the spectrum. In particular, DMC 316 and 3726, which are from the same colour range, and can both look rather dull and lifeless, particularly compared with other more vivid hues. However, when they are placed on an ecru background, they simply glow with warmth, whereas a brighter and more intense shade would dominate and subdue the surrounding colour scheme.

DMC 407 is a lovely soft pink that blends perfectly with other colours, and also makes an ideal flesh-colour for the figures. Although on the chart it appears quite dark compared to the paler shades in the same range, which initially seem more suited for the task, these paler colours would in fact disappear and look almost white, once they were competing with the rest of the design. This is a typical example of a colour that you would imagine to be the correct shade, when selecting it as a possible skin-tone from the colour chart, but one that ultimately would not work successfully on the embroidery.

DMC 632 AND ANCHOR 936

I find that these two deep-rust colours are frequently required, particularly when portraying birds, which often include small amounts of the colour red, and the addition of one strand of this muted shade will take the edge off a bright red. I have also found both these colours work very well as one of the red tones in a building; either to help make a brick-colour or combined with a dull green, to express a tile-colour on a roof.

ANCHOR 13

This is a true pillar-box red and ideal for illustrating the splashes of red found on wild birds and poultry. As the amounts of red involved may only be small flecks, it will depend very much on the surrounding colour scheme as to whether or not the colour is toned down, with either rust red Anchor 936 or perhaps brown DMC 434.

Blue

ANCHOR 920, 921 AND 922

I love using blue in a design and will look for any excuse to incorporate it somewhere, however small the motif. Just the addition of a tiny blue butterfly in an area of earthy browns and yellows will bring a whole new focus to the design. Also, blues and creams alongside each other are an ideal match, with each varying shade of blue conveying a different mood. I have included quite a range in my designs, particularly for the water areas, but the three colours listed above seem to co-ordinate perfectly with all the other colours in my basic palette. I have, on many occasions, looked for this group on the colour chart and not been able to find them, as they appear so dull and dreary alongside the other blues. However, once they are in place on the embroidery they simply glow with intensity and convey a sense of harmony to the whole composition.

Green

DMC 503–500, 320, 3347 AND ANCHOR 216

The numerous variables involved in depicting natural elements, such as trees, grasses and plants, make the use of greens a far more complex subject. As this colour has a very wide spectrum, ranging from a turquoise shade in the blue end, to a pale olive at the yellow end, the amount of choices and possibilities can seem quite overwhelming. I have found several different greens that I use repeatedly throughout my designs, as I feel very comfortable with them and I have come to know exactly how they will work in conjunction with many other colours. The group of blue/greens, DMC 503–500, graduating from light to dark, have a wonderful knack of blending in with almost any situation, and masquerade as feathers or water just as easily as suggesting pine-needles. DMC 320 and Anchor 216 are very similar mid-greens but I find their individual characteristics make them indispensable. DMC 3347 on the other hand is more of a yellow/green and excellent for highlighting a blend of colours or used as a single strand to depict blades of grass. There are many other shades of green that I could mention, some of which you will come across in the projects, and once you have become familiar with a number of them you will develop your own particular preferences.

Fabrics

One of the most noticeable aspects of the traditional sampler is the sympathetic marriage of colours between the background cloth and the muted tones of the natural dyed threads, giving a sense of harmony and balance to the whole embroidery. Through circumstance rather than by choice, the majority of fabrics available to the needle-worker prior to the nineteenth century would have been presented in an unbleached state and subject to considerable variations in quality. This would account for the many subtle shades of brown, beige and yellow, that are so common in early examples. Even the limited amount of cloth that was put through a bleaching process, and probably had the appearance of being white, would in fact have been quite dull and discoloured by today's standards. The materials most commonly used for sampler embroidery were selected from a range of linens, varying in weight and texture from a very fine count to a much coarser heavier weave. At a later date a woollen Tammy cloth, with a more open weave, became popular as it was easier to work, but it was not as hard wearing and was so prone to being attacked by moths that it was eventually abandoned. Delicate fabrics such as silk, were usually backed with linen to give them strength and reserved for specially designed pictorial embroideries, rather than practise pieces.

By the early nineteenth century, the introduction of chemical dyes brought a completely new range of vivid colours onto the market, and at about the same time new methods of bleaching cloth made it possible for a pure white fabric to be mass-produced at an affordable price. These two important changes caused great excitement and much interest and were soon incorporated into all the latest designs and patterns.

Within a short space of time, a whole colour scheme, which had been used for generations, was rejected. The soft, earthy hues of the natural dyes and fabrics were replaced by a palette of very bright and vibrant colours, which were now considered essential to creating a modern piece of work.

Even today, the preference for using a white ground with shades of primary colours is still a popular choice. Throughout the twentieth century, many projects have been designed around this type of colour scheme, and often only suggest using more subdued shades of fabrics and threads when the pattern is in the style of a traditional sampler. We have now become so accustomed to being surrounded by bright colours and dazzling whites, that the idea of muted colours being associated with an old-fashioned look has evolved. As a colour, white is very dominant, and I find it can cause various problems when planning a colour scheme for an embroidery. The very whiteness of the fabric has a tendency to drain the colour from any threads placed on it, and rather than enhancing a design, the colours will actually take on a dull and lifeless appearance, making it necessary to use ever brighter shades to achieve a colourful result. Another drawback of embroidering onto a white ground is the difficulty in working successfully with threads of lighter shades, particularly in the range of creams and off-whites, as they will merge so easily into the background. Many of the lighter colours, far from appearing pastel and washed-out, can in fact bring a wonderful lustrous quality to the work, when used on the various tones of natural coloured fabrics.

My personal choice of colours has always inclined towards the softer more earthy hues, and by using fabrics from this colour range I feel that the background becomes a more considered part of the design, and gives a greater feeling of unity to the overall embroidery. I have, therefore, decided to use a variety of off-white fabrics for all the projects in the book, and I hope that you will find them as exciting and satisfying to use, as I do myself. If you have never previously worked on an ecru-coloured fabric, you may feel that some of them have the appearance of being rather dull and gloomy. However, once you begin to embroider your design, the colours of the motifs will become the focal point of interest, and the background will begin to appear much lighter and less noticeable.

When making your own embroidery designs, your choice of fabric will be influenced by the type of subject you have in mind and the various colours needed to portray it. For instance, whether a building is constructed of brick, flint, stone or perhaps painted white will have much significance; as will the colours of any wildlife, pets, trees, flowers or other motifs. Once you have decided on the main elements to be included in the design, pick out three or four of the predominant colours, and lay the skeins on several different shades of fabric until you find a combination of ground colour and threads that complement each other. Sometimes it will be necessary to change a shade of one of the coloured threads, perhaps exchanging a white/cream for a yellow/cream, or perhaps a blue/green might blend more harmoniously than a leaf green. It is easy to play around with the colours at this stage, and therefore worth spending some time trying out various combinations, until you feel the colours look right.

Besides the colour of the fabric, the other important consideration is the type and weight of the weave. All cross-stitch embroidery should be worked on evenweave fabrics, as this ensures that all the stitches are a regular size and this makes it easier to follow the patterns. Traditionally, linen has always been thought of as the superior fabric, and its beautiful qualities combined with its durability over the centuries has earned it the reputation of being the best choice for an embroidery. However, in spite of its excellent characteristics, linen has a tendency to produce a slubby texture in the weave, which can make it quite difficult to see the holes clearly. I personally find it quite taxing on the eyes, and there is nothing more frustrating than having to struggle with each stitch. Unless you are already experienced with linen fabrics, I would advise you to experiment on a small off-cut before committing yourself to a large project. Today there is a whole new range of fabrics that have proved to be excellent alternatives and which have a more uniform weave, making them much easier to work with.

Fabric Information

I have used Evenweave and Aida fabrics for the following projects, and all the designs are compatible on both types of fabric. The Zweigart company produces a wide selection of fabrics, with a good cross-match of colours between the various ranges. The different weights of cloth are indicated by a count number, with higher codes corresponding to the finer weaves. The most popular choices are Evenweave 25–28 count and Aida 14 count. Some of the fabrics are sold as packaged 'cut-pieces', which are ideal for the following projects, otherwise they can be purchased as lengths cut from the roll. Occasionally, some of the colours from certain fabric ranges may be temporarily unavailable or will have been exchanged for a slightly different shade. Should you have any problems or queries, please contact your nearest stockist, or DMC Creative World directly. There are a number of addresses at the end of the book.

Zweigart Fabrics

BRITTNEY E3270 28 COUNT: 52 PER CENT COTTON/48 PER CENT RAYON
A lovely range of colours and an easy regular weave, which is very workable. I have used this fabric many times with excellent results.

CASHEL LINEN E3281 28 COUNT: 100 PER CENT LINEN

A wide range of natural and dyed colours. The texture is slightly slubby with a more compact weave, but has a beautiful quality.

LINDA E1235 27 COUNT: 100 PER CENT COTTON

A smaller colour range but a lovely fabric to work with, and the weave is noticeably more open.

LUGANA E3835 25 COUNT: 52 PER CENT COTTON/48 PER CENT RAYON

An excellent fabric with a wide range of subtle colours. The weave is extremely easy to see and the fabric handles beautifully.

AIDA E3706 14 COUNT: 100 PER CENT COTTON

These fabrics have been woven in such a way that the threads form small squares, making it very easy to count the holes in between. Zweigart produce a wide range of colours in a variety of counts including 18, 16, 14 and 11. The most popular for cross-stitch is usually 14, and the results are very similar to a 28 count Evenweave, but much easier to work.

Threads

I have always referred to my skeins of embroidery threads as 'silks' and this seems to be a very common term, used by many needle-workers to this day. The fact that the majority of early samplers were worked entirely in silk is maybe one of the reasons for this misconception arising. Besides which, the beautiful quality and lustre of the threads today so closely resembles the properties of silk, that it belies the fact that they are actually made from stranded cotton.

The two main producers of embroidery threads are DMC and Anchor, with both companies covering a wide colour spectrum and including a wonderful range of shades in every hue. The many subtle differences between the two companies provides an enormous choice for the embroiderer, and I have selected particular colours from each range, which I feel ideally complement and enhance each another. There are full colour charts available for viewing at most stockists, and it is worth taking the time to browse through them, as it can be difficult to appreciate all the subtle variations in the shades when the skeins are hanging on the rails. If you are a keen needle-worker or belong to a group, you might consider buying copies of the charts for your own use, as they are invaluable when designing a project yourself.

The skein itself consists of a main thread, which in turn is made up of six strands; these need to be separated out before you begin to embroider as this helps the threads to lay more evenly and also makes for a fuller stitch with more body. There are a number of factors that will influence the amount of threads you decide to use at one time; in particular, the count of the fabric, as the thickness of the threads has to be compatible with the count of the weave. Also the various effects you wish to achieve will determine whether you should use one, two or three threads, and occasionally I have even used four, in order to make a specific colour. The average length of thread for your needle should be about 18in (46cm); anything shorter will run out too quickly, and longer threads will end up looking worn and fluffy. Sometimes a thread can start to look very thin and tired before you have reached the end of the length, in which case immediately stop working and start anew, otherwise the stitches will look very dull and lifeless compared to the others.

Throughout the following projects I have used either two or three threads of different shades to make up the colours for the individual motifs, and organizing the colours into their respective groups will save time and frustration when you are working. I find the best solution is to keep each set of skeins in a clear plastic bag, together with the cut lengths, so they can be easily identified. Quite often the small wrapper bearing the colour-code will slip off the skein, and should this happen Sellotape it back on straight away, as once the colour has become separated from its dye code it can be very difficult to match it. When I have finished a particular project, I always try to re-organize all the threads into colour groups, as this makes it much easier to begin the next piece of work.

Needles

Everyone has a favourite needle, which feels comfortable to handle; many embroiderers prefer to work with a rounded end, as it is kinder on the fingers. Needles with a blunt end are basically designed for tapestry work, although they are quite suitable for working cross-stitch as long as they are slim enough to pass through the fabric easily. However, you will need to change to a different style of needle when beginning the overstitched areas. An embroidery or crewel needle with a sharp point is essential, to avoid damaging the existing threads and fabric, as you rework the original stitches. Also, you will find that needles with a long flat eye will be easier and quicker to thread.

The recommended needle size is 24 Tapestry and 5 Embroidery/Crewel.

Hoops and Frames

It is actually just as easy to work the embroidery in your hands as it is to work with the fabric supported in a hoop or frame. The raised surfaces and delicate stitches I use in my designs are very susceptible to pressure, and I have now become accustomed to working without a frame and simply supporting the embroidery on a cushion, placed on my lap. I have never encountered any problems with misshapen or distorted fabrics once the work is finished, and in fact find the freedom to manipulate the material as I am working very helpful.

If you enjoy working with a hoop frame, you can certainly make use of the expanding sizes when working on a large project, but you will really need to discard them once the embroidery no longer fits within the area. The remainder of the design must now be worked without the frame, as the stitches will lose their sheen and brilliance if they are crushed between the two hoops, and the final effect of your work will be spoilt.

The other possibility is to use a rectangular wooden frame, and these are fine if you are familiar with them. Alternatively, you could try a plastic interlocking frame, which is easier to set up and has the advantage of being collapsible, which would allow you to temporarily remove your work at any time.

Stitches

The great diversity of embroidery stitches in use during the early seventeenth century were on the whole variations on a theme, involving three basic techniques: straight-stitches, loops and knots. The many band samplers of this period reveal decorative patterns that exhibit two main characteristics: one focusing on the construction of the stitch to form a textural pattern, and the other making use of a simple stitch to describe a two-dimensional image. The style of work involving intricate stitch combinations were, in the main, practised on samplers for later use in decorating and edging garments and household linen. However, the formal and repetitive format required in the construction of the stitch posed certain limitations on creating an individual statement, whereas simpler techniques, such as running-stitch or cross-stitch, allowed for greater scope and flexibility and were more suited for portraying motifs and designs. Gradually, the desire for more pictorial samplers grew, and the variety of stitches decreased as the subject matter and illustration of motifs became more important. Also, the particular style of the embroidery stitch would often be dictated by the weave of the cloth, as some fabrics were very fine and with an irregular weave, which would make the use of cross-stitch a most laborious task. In these circumstances it was more practical to outline the main motifs in a running-stitch or back-stitch and then fill in these areas with small straight-stitches, which were laid together to form a textural surface following the direction of the form. The text and borders would then be worked in cross-stitch, quite often as a very fine petit point, using a single thread. As needlework became a compulsory part of a child's education, the amount of individual choice allowed in the composition of the embroidery would have depended very much on the inclinations of the particular schoolmistress. Small private schools probably had far more freedom to encourage creative expression amongst their pupils, and perhaps this accounts for some of the highly imaginative and original examples that were produced during the eighteenth and early nineteenth centuries. Unfortunately, the sampler was eventually reduced to a schoolroom exercise, with cross-stitch as the single technique, as all importance was placed on each child completing a neat piece of work, rather than an artistic image.

Stitch Techniques

The types of stitches you decide to include in an embroidery will be influenced by the nature of your subject matter and the kind of effects you wish to achieve. Although there are a wide range of techniques for creating a variety of decorative stitches, I have found that the simpler the stitch, the more versatile its possibilities. An embroidery stitch that is very intricate in its construction will draw attention to its own decorative qualities, and will not necessarily help to complement and describe a pictorial form. Your choice of stitch needs to be matched to the motifs or subject you are planning to illustrate. I have listed several basic techniques, which I use throughout the projects, and that are probably already quite familiar to the majority of needle-workers.

CROSS-STITCH
The simplicity and ease with which this stitch can be worked has meant that it can be mastered very quickly. Its even and uniform appearance has made it an ideal technique for portraying formal structures such as buildings, the angular patterns of letterforms and also repetitive, stylized borders. The very squareness of the outlines lends a distinctive charm to the embroidery and can transform any subject into a decorative motif. In recent years it has become popular to disguise the stepped pattern of a cross-stitch motif by using half-stitches to round off the edges. Although this is a useful technique on certain occasions, I feel that on the whole, it is a shame to detract from the characteristic qualities of the stitch, and have found that the pronounced angular edges can be softened through the use of colour mixing and blending.

Stitch Techniques

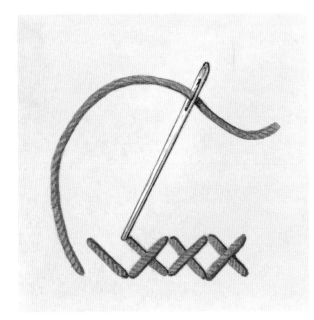

Cross-stitch. Either worked individually or as rows of half crosses, which are worked first in one direction and then reworked to form the complete cross. All the stitches should face in the same direction, unless otherwise indicated in the pattern.

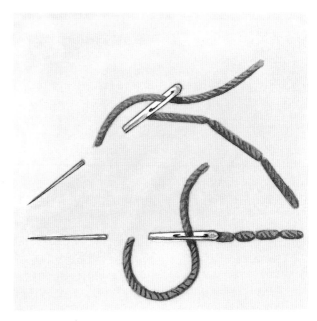

Back-stitch. This basic stitch is made up of a series of evenly sized stitches and usually outlines a cross-stitch motif. The longer version of the stitch has more possibilities and the length of each stitch is indicated by a series of dots on the graph patterns.

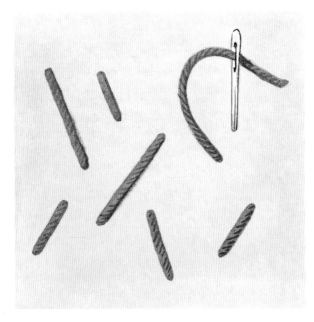

Straight-stitch. These randomly placed stitches can be made to any length and follow any direction. They can either be laid next to each other to completely cover an area or crossed over one another to build up a dense textural surface.

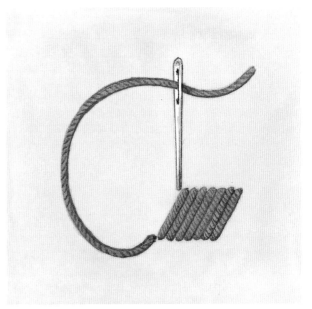

Satin-stitch. The stitches should all follow the same direction and lay close enough together to cover the background fabric completely. Never make a stitch so long that it begins to slack, and any large areas to be covered should be divided into smaller sections.

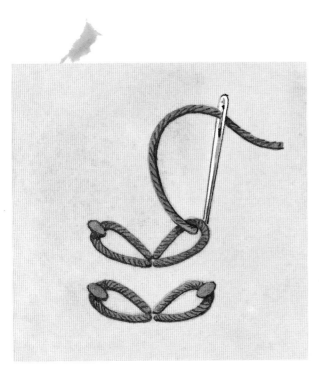

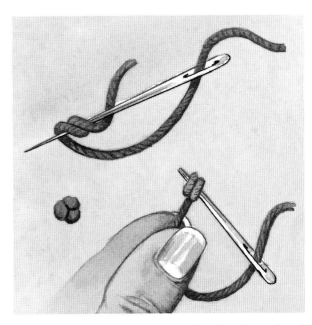

Lazy-daisy. This stitch is always very delicate in appearance and usually worked with one or two threads. The length of the stitch can be varied slightly but the little tie-down loop at the top should be kept as small as possible.

French-knots. The size of this stitch will depend on the number of threads you use and the how many times you wind the thread round the needle. It also helps to twist the threads slightly, so that the threads make a closed knot and do not splay apart.

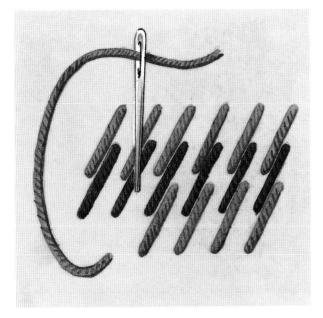

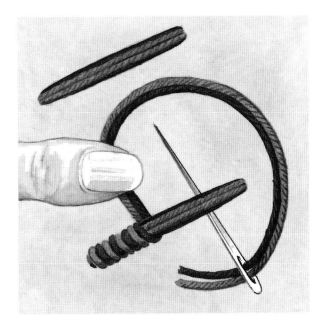

Slanting-stitch. This stitch always covers a cross-stitch base and is worked in a stepped format. The diagonal stitches are worked over four cross-stitch squares, moving along from right to left, starting on every stitch. The second line begins on the next row down of cross-stitches, and the third line of stitches share the same hole as the bottom of the first stitch, with the second stitch separating them. I find it easiest to begin each line at the right, and work across the motif in the same direction.

Roll-stitch. Make a knot in the end of your thread and bring the needle up from the back of the fabric, just catching the weave of the cloth, so that the thread does not pull through. Make a straight stitch to the required length and repeat, to make a double stitch. Bring the needle back to the beginning, and work a series of roll-stitches, being careful to keep the threads untwisted. If you hold each new loop in place with your thumb, it will stop the threads from slipping out of order.

BACK-STITCH

This is an ideal stitch for outlining forms and defining edges between two areas of colour. It is also particularly useful as a way of accentuating a cross-stitch motif, by following the outline of the form in a contrasting colour. The stitch can be worked to any length, and as a linear free-flowing line it has many possibilities and can be used to draw quite accurately on the fabric. This method of working makes it very easy to transfer fairly complex designs onto a chart, plotting the graph to coincide with the holes in the fabric, as for instance in the Jug of Tulips pattern.

STRAIGHT-STITCH OR LONG- AND SHORT-STITCHES

I find this is the most versatile and expressive of stitches, as it can be made to any length and worked in any direction. The random application and variable sizes of the stitch, combined with the relevant colour for a particular motif, allows for a highly suggestive interpretation of any subject. This style of working calls for a more artistic approach, since there are no precise patterns for the arrangement of the stitches, with each needle-worker creating an original piece of embroidery.

SATIN-STITCH

This is another version of straight-stitch, only in this case the stitches are laid beside each other in a slanted or upright direction, to build up a smooth textural surface. This has always been a favourite sampler stitch, and is often used to fill in small motifs that have been outlined in back-stitch. On other occasions the stitches might be arranged in rows to cover a larger area, such as for grasses or water, and the wonderful lustrous sheen that this creates is always most appealing.

RANDOM SATIN-STITCH (not illustrated)

This is a combination of the long-stitch and satin-stitch techniques and is used to build up a heavily textured surface. Small stitches of varying lengths are closely packed together to completely cover an area, usually following the outline of the motif.

LAZY-DAISY

This is a very attractive stitch that closely resembles a naturalistic structure, making it ideal for illustrating a variety of subjects. It is an excellent technique for suggesting leaf shapes, and I have found it works perfectly when depicting the ears of corn in the wheat border. The use of two different tones of thread, combined with the natural twist and fall of the threads as you work, will create a random effect with the colours, conjuring a sense of light and movement in the design.

FRENCH-KNOTS

This is a very decorative stitch with a distinctive form, which is ideal for interpreting certain subjects, but on the whole it has a more limited application. This small stitch can be varied in size to some degree and is usually a very neat, closed structure. However, it is possible to improvise on the basic technique and make a much larger more open stitch, which is very useful for creating textural surfaces. I have done just this, to suggest the rough woollen coats of the Suffolk sheep, to great effect.

SLANTING-STITCH

This is a technique that I have devised, which creates a real and applied textural surface to a motif, while at the same time disguising the structure of the cross-stitch. It is really a form of satin-stitch and has a similar silky sheen, only the stitches are arranged in a stepped format and are not so densely packed together. The technique has a wide range of possibilities, particularly as you can make use of the colour combinations between the two surfaces to create an exciting mix of light and dark tones.

ROLL-STITCH

This is similar to bullion-stitch and has a very three-dimensional structure. I prefer to use this particular technique, as I feel it is more controlled than a bullion-stitch, and therefore easier to work small details accurately. The size of the stitch can be varied in both the length and the thickness, and I have found this the perfect technique for depicting bees and dragonflies. It can also be used in a more random manner and, for example, makes a wonderful surface texture that closely resembles sheep's wool.

Preparing to Work

◆ Once you have chosen your fabric and cut it to the correct size, allowing at least a 3–4in (8–11cm) margin round the design, you will need to bind the edges of the fabric to stop it from fraying as you work. The easiest and quickest method is to cover the raw edges with masking tape and then add some staples about every 6in (16cm) to secure the tape firmly in place and prevent it from working loose.

◆ At this stage you may need to iron the fabric, should it have any creases. Some of the pre-cut pieces are packaged with a fold down the centre, and a damp cloth and hot iron will usually flatten it out. However, do not worry if you can still see traces of the fold, you will find it disappears completely when the finished work is stretched, as will any creases that arise from handling the fabric as you work.

◆ I must mention here, and I will again in the section on mounting work, please never iron your finished embroidery. Once the stitches are flattened, not only will they lose their lustre, but the delicate raised surface of the stitches will be totally destroyed.

◆ The next step is to work some tacking stitches onto the fabric, as guide-lines for the design. Most embroiderers have their own system for marking out the fabric, with the centre of the design probably being the usual choice, although beginning from the top and working down the design is another popular method. However, I always prefer to make my guide-lines along the edges of the design, as this enables me to plot out the small divisional borders, which feature in all the large projects, and use them as reference points to centre the other motifs. It does not really matter which method you use, as long as you have allowed enough fabric for framing the embroidery.

Marking Out the Fabric

There are measurements for the finished designs and fabric sizes on the project pages, but if you are planning to extend the designs or work from your own design, remember to allow enough extra fabric for mounting the embroidery. The smaller projects can be marked out quite easily in any method you prefer, but you might like to try this alternative approach for the larger projects in the book. Measure in 4¾in (12cm) from the bottom edge and right-

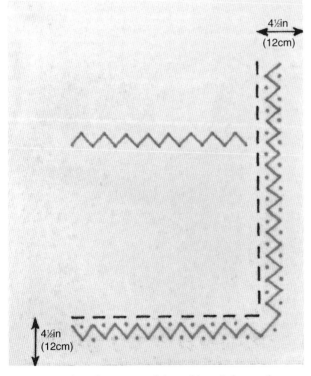

4½in
(12cm)

4½in
(12cm)

Diagram to show the position of the tacking stitches on the fabric, with the borders outlined in blue.

hand side of the fabric and mark temporarily with a pin. Then, using a mid-coloured thread, work a line of tacking stitches, counting accurately over two and under two cross-stitch squares, in both a vertical and horizontal direction, for the lengths of the graph patterns. With these evenly spaced stitches in place, it is easy to match the graphs to the fabric and begin to plot the design. These tram-lines are just inside the outer border and can be used as a guide to place the narrow band borders across the design, which then makes it very easy to position all the motifs. Once you feel you have built up enough references, the guide-lines can be removed.

Beginning to Sew

There are no rules about where you should start working, but I usually leave the outer borders until the end and begin with one of the larger motifs, such as a building or tree. If you use the vertical tram-line as a guide to positioning the narrow borders on the fabric, it will then be much easier to place the various motifs that run along them. In this way, you are not committed to finishing any particular area before you move on to the next, but will be free to build up the design as you wish. I always try to work as many of the cross-stitch areas as possible, before I start to rework the motifs that need overstitching, so as to avoid crushing the delicate surfaces and spoiling the lustrous quality of the threads.

First Stitches

Now you are ready to begin sewing and the first stitch of any individual motif needs to be secured carefully. Bring the needle through from the back of the fabric, leaving an end of about 1in (3cm), and hold this in place as you make the first stitch. Work at least four more stitches, being sure to catch in the loose thread. Once you have worked an area of embroidery, you can begin any new threads and finish them off by running the needle through the back of the stitches. The length of thread you work with should be no more than 18in (46cm), and you will find it helpful to try and cut the different colours to the same length, as this will make it quicker to put together the various colour combinations.

Following the Patterns

I have tried to make the graph patterns as simple as possible, with many of the motifs requiring only an outline to describe them. However, the patterns for the birds are slightly more complicated, requiring several colour changes, and I have used symbols on the graphs with a corresponding colour key. The back-stitch lines that travel round the edge of the cross-stitch shapes are shown as a dark outline. The longer back-stitch lines either describe a form, as in the tulip design, or single line of stitching, as in the fir-branches. These are all shown as a single line punctuated with small dots, which represent the length of each stitch.

Stitch Directions and Colour Mixing

◆ All the cross-stitches are worked with the top stitch slanting to the right, except where the patterns suggest a change. The symbol \ in the instructions, indicates a change in direction, and on these occasions the top stitch of the cross-stitch will slant to the left.

◆ The majority of the colours are made up of a combination of shades, using two or three different-coloured threads in the needle together. The amounts for each colour are indicated in the brackets, alongside the colour code.

Tension: Stitches in Relation to Fabric

The tension of your work will depend to a certain extent on how tightly you pull your thread after each stitch, as a series of stitches that are too compact will cause the fabric to pull in, whereas an area of loose stitches will make little pleats in the surface. However, most people very quickly build up an even and regular rhythm of working, and any little discrepancies that occur are usually sorted out when the embroidery is mounted. Another factor is the compatibility of the fabric to the number of threads in the needle. Many early samplers were worked entirely in petit point, as the linens were so fine that only a single thread could be used, and a fabric with a close weave, such as a 31 count linen, will be limited to one or two threads at the most. I have mainly worked with 28 count fabrics, and although this is often considered best suited to two threads, I have always managed to use three threads quite successfully. All the following projects are worked on either 14 count Aida or 25 count Evenweave, and both fabrics are quite happy with three threads. However, it does help to spread the tension by alternating between the two weights of thread, so that some motifs are worked in two threads and others in three. This can be very useful when covering a large area such as a building, where you need to take care that such a concentrated area of stitches does not cause the motif to pull in at the edges. The use of three threads for the walls of the building and then only two threads across the roof area, would help to balance the tension. Similarly, a motif that requires

a heavy amount of overstitching, such as a grass or water area, would benefit from having a cross-stitch base that is worked in just two threads. When working on a motif that covers a large expanse of cross-stitch, I find it helpful to divide the pattern into sections and work small areas at a time. By staggering the lines at the end of each row of stitches, it is possible to connect the two areas without creating a hard edge in the embroidery. I have described this method further in the directions for making up the meadow grass.

Making Corrections

Even the most experienced embroiderer can encounter a problem that needs correcting, whether it is the necessity to change a colour, or alter the shape of a motif. The most common mistake is miscounting the stitches and finding that you have been working in the wrong area, as even one stitch out of place can sometimes make all the difference to the design.

Obviously, the easiest solution is to get into the habit of frequently checking your work against the pattern, so that any errors are discovered at an early stage. In the event of finding a mistake, a few minutes unpicking a small section is well worth the effort, even though it may seem a terrible nuisance at the time; but do remember to begin with a new thread and not re-use a thread that looks worn. However, the fault may be too far back in a border pattern for instance, or in an awkward position that will require disturbing other areas of the embroidery. Then the simplest answer is to carefully cut the top thread of the cross-stitch that lies in the centre of the problem, and unpick a few stitches either side of it. Some of the stitches may need the underside of the cross-stitch unpicked first, depending on the direction they were originally worked. Once you have freed a small amount of thread on each side, pull it through to the back of the embroidery and, with a single thread of the same colour, overstitch the loose ends securely. I have even used this strategy quite successfully on a single stitch that has been out of place. Since samplers are never washed or used in a functional manner, there is little risk of any short ends working loose, and if you have any doubts just overstitch any adjacent stitches at the back of the embroidery, in a singe thread of the same colour.

However, sometimes it is the choice of colour that is the cause of the trouble, whether it be simply that a colour no longer looks right, or just that you inadvertently used the wrong shade. In most cases, rather than unpicking the embroidery, it is possible to rework the area with either a full cross-stitch or a half cross-stitch, using one or sometimes two threads. Obviously the degree of colour change required will influence your decisions and determine the number

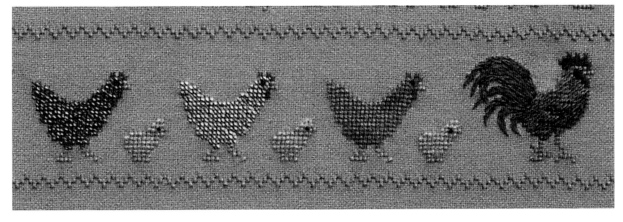

Hens and cockerel from Mill Farm sampler.

of threads you will need. I have occasionally used three threads and reworked a full cross-stitch to cover a particular colour. Although that piece of stitching may look a bit raised at the time, it always merges quite successfully in the end, as the stitches will flatten out, simply from handling the fabric as you continue working.

Borders have a reputation for being an area where problems can easily arise, and you really do need to glance back over your work about every twenty stitches and check with your pattern. As this is often the final part of the design to be worked, it is tempting to begin rushing and make a miscalculation in your eagerness to finish the piece. The majority of border designs are arranged in a formal style, which rely on a symmetrical repeat pattern, so even one stitch out of place will result in a border that does not match. If the fault has gone undetected you will need to find it and consider how much work it will involve to unpick back to that stage. However, you may feel you cannot face the effort, especially if the pattern is quite detailed and intricate, in which case you could try the following suggestion. Borders are quite tricky to correct, but it is possible to try and disguise the mistake by re-organizing parts of the pattern so that the fault will be less noticeable. You may need to unpick a small area of the design and then re-stitch it to include a cross-stitch that runs over three threads (covering one-and-a-half cross-stitches). By calculating how many of these stitches you need to include, you can then shorten or lengthen the design at appropriate intervals so that you can achieve a neat join. The slightly larger cross-stitches will soon blend into the pattern and you will hardly notice them after a while.

Lettering can also present similar problems, especially if it has to fit into a particular area. It can be very easy to misjudge the spacing and for this reason I often work any lettering from both ends at the same time, so that I am certain that the first and last words will definitely fit. If you then find any differences you can extend or shorten a word by using a cross-stitch that runs over one thread (half a cross-stitch), and include them in the letter forms where they will be least noticed.

Many mistakes that appear disastrous to you at the time, will actually go unnoticed by anyone else, and can even be quite difficult for you to spot once the embroidery is finished. Many of the traditional samplers were full of little mistakes, particularly those made by children, but this all adds to their overall charm. It is the individual variations of each stitch that give handmade embroideries their special qualities, and they should not be compared to the uniformity of a machine product.

Framing

It is usually best to take your finished embroidery to a professional picture framer unless you are already experienced in mounting and framing the work yourself. However, there are a few points to remember when preparing the work and choosing the frame.

First, a sampler embroidery should never be ironed, as this will damage the delicate raised surfaces of the stitches and also spoil the lustre of the threads. I know that many needle-workers rush to flatten out their designs in this way, but the heat and pressure of the iron will affect even a basic cross-stitch, and would certainly ruin the quality of particular motifs with a very textural surface. Any creases in the fabric will be pulled taught when the embroidery is stretched in the mounting process.

The next point that must be mentioned is to be sure that only acid-free card is used for mounting the embroidery.

Another consideration is the frame itself, as you will need to choose a style that has a deep enough setting to allow for the insert of a wooden strip between the frame and the embroidery, which keeps the glass supported away from the surface of the work. I usually frame my pieces in maple and use a gold-leaf slip, which gives a very traditional look to the work.

And lastly you will need to find a suitable spot to hang your framed sampler, as direct sunlight will gradually damage the threads and fade the colours.

2 Fruit and Flower Arrangements

The decorative arrangement of fruits and flowers in various styles of bowls, baskets or urns appears in so many samplers that it must surely have been one of the most popular embroidery subjects throughout the eighteenth and nineteenth centuries. The most common and frequently used motif displayed a symmetrical pattern of fruit placed in a pyramid formation, ranging in scale from a small dish containing six or eight fruits to more elaborate centrepieces including fifteen or more fruits. In these particular designs, the fruit was always portrayed in very simple geometric shapes, being worked entirely in cross-stitch, and became a favourite choice of motif amongst the schoolroom samplers. These small and attractive stylized designs were obviously a very easy and effective way of filling in any odd empty spaces, and also provided the opportunity to use a wide range of random colour schemes.

The arrangements of flowers, on the other hand, allowed more scope for a naturalistic and artistic interpretation, and there are many beautiful examples of highly complex and elaborate compositions. This style of work was much more common during the early eighteenth century, when the use of a wide range of stitches and techniques made it possible to create a richly textured and intricate embroidery. The American tradition embraced this particular subject throughout its history, and produced some beautiful examples of flower arrangements that were quite often the focal point of the whole embroidery. However, with the advent of sampler embroidery becoming predominantly a classroom activity, and the gradual move towards cross-stitch as the main technique, these complex designs were eventually adapted and simplified, to include a more formal and stylized pattern of flower.

The whole subject of floral arrangements provides a wealth of ideas and inspiration, which makes it an excellent theme for a sampler to commemorate any number of occasions. The baskets, jardinières, jugs or vases lend themselves perfectly to interpretation in embroidery, with the possibility of creating infinite variations through the use of pattern, texture and colour. I have designed a number of compositions that could either form the focal point of an embroidery or, equally effectively, feature in a larger piece of work. The following projects all have a decorative display as the central theme and have been designed to fit within a similar size of border, making it possible to mix and match the different styles of borders and motifs. In a small piece of work there is sometimes only a limited space in which to include all the necessary information, and my suggestions for combining the various patterns of lettering together with an attractive composition will hopefully inspire you to develop your own personal designs.

This detail illustrates the three stages involved in building up the tulip design.

Basket of Fruit

This attractive basket of fruit echoes the traditional pyramid style of motif, and would make an ideal subject for a sampler to commemorate a wedding or anniversary. I have suggested a group of colours to depict the various fruits, but you could easily alter the colour scheme, either to suit a particular occasion or simply as a way of using up any threads you have available. The design is basically worked in cross-stitch, but I decided to overstitch the fruits with a slanting-stitch, so as to soften the uniform nature of the stitch and to create a silky texture that helps to distinguish them from the rest of the design.

Materials Guide

◆ *See* 'Preparing to Work', page 18.
◆ Zweigart fabrics are quoted for all projects.

FABRICS
Aida 14 count Summer Khaki
Lugana 25 count Pewter
Fabric size approximately 11 × 13in (29 × 34cm)
Design size approximately 6 × 7in (15 × 19cm)
Stitch count 73 × 97

THREADS
DMC and Anchor:
Green – DMC 501, 502, 3052
Blue – Anchor 920, 921, 922
White – DMC 746, 3047
Yellow – DMC 782, 783
Orange – DMC 976

Pink – DMC 316, 356, 3041, 3721, 3726, 3740,
Anchor 349

◆ Find centre of fabric and begin with large fruit A.
◆ The amounts of threads for each colour combination are indicated in brackets (*see* page 20).
◆ The alphabet for this design is no. 6 (*see* page 121).

◆ Work the whole design in cross-stitch and then rework the fruits in slanitng-stitch, using a single thread of the same colour.

BASKET
Blue lines – Anchor 921 (3)
Blue spots – Anchor 922 (3)
White – DMC 3047 (3)
Feet – Anchor 921 (2), Anchor 922 (1)

FRUIT
A – DMC 783 (3)
B – DMC 976 (3)
C – Anchor 349 (3)
D – DMC 782 (3)
E – DMC 3740 (3)
F – DMC 3721 (3)
G – DMC 356 (3)
H – DMC 316 (3)
J – DMC 3726 (3)
K – DMC 3041(3)

LEAVES
DMC 502 (2), DMC 3052 (1)

STEMS
DMC 501 (3)

BORDERS
Work in cross-stitch:
White – DMC 3047 (2), DMC 746 (1)
Pink – DMC 316 (3)

In this detail from a larger sampler, I have worked the basket in an alternative colour scheme, and added a traditional border pattern to widen the design and accommodate a longer piece of text.

BIRDS
Left bird / stitch direction
Right bird \ stitch direction
Birds – Anchor 921 (1), Anchor 920 (1)
Beak – Anchor 922 (2)
Eye – DMC 3721 (2) – French-knot
Leaves – DMC 502 (1), DMC 3052 (1)
Stem – DMC 501 (1) – back-stitch

LETTERING
Work in back-stitch:
Text – Anchor 922 (1)

Lavender

Throughout the Middle Ages lavender was used mainly for medicinal and culinary purposes and was cultivated as a kitchen herb rather than a garden flower, although when Henry VIII decided to plant out his castle gardens with beds of lavender, the hitherto humble flower gained a new status and popularity. And yet, in spite of its common usage in all walks of life, I can find no references to it in any examples of needlework from this age or later. This could have been for the very reason that it was considered an insignificant and common plant, or alternatively that its structure was not as decorative and flamboyant as a rose or carnation and therefore would not make such an impressive motif. However, since the later half of the twentieth century, with the renewed interest in all forms of arts and crafts, stylized interpretations of this pretty little flower have been used in many needlework designs.

Materials Guide

◆ *See* 'Preparing to Work', page 18.
◆ Zweigart fabrics are quoted for all projects.

FABRIC
Aida 14 count Antique
Lugana 25 count Fawn
Design size approximately 3¾ × 3in (9.5 × 8cm)

THREADS
DMC and Anchor:
Yellow – DMC 676, 729, 782, 434, 433
Green – DMC 320
Purple/pink – DMC 792, 340
      Anchor 870, 87, 112
White – Anchor 300

The picturesque ideal of a country cottage always includes a garden path edged with rows of lavender, and I felt I just had to include a decorative arrangement of this favourite flower. I chose a warm-coloured fabric to work on, as it set off the mauves and purples to their best effect and also complimented the golden colours in the basketwork. Once again, the finished embroidery has the appearance of being very complicated to execute, but in fact it only involves the use of four different stitches: cross-stitch, back-stitch, lazy-daisy and French-knot, and by following the various stages illustrated here, the design is surprisingly simple to make up.

◆ Follow the graphs to build up the flowers and patterns on the basket. The light green on the stems looks quite pale initially, but it will appear much brighter once the lavender colours are in place.

STEP 1
BASKET
Work in cross-stitch:
DMC 782 (1), DMC 729 (1), DMC 676 (1)

STEMS
Work in long back-stitch – the dots on the graph indicate the length of the stitch:
DMC 320 (1)

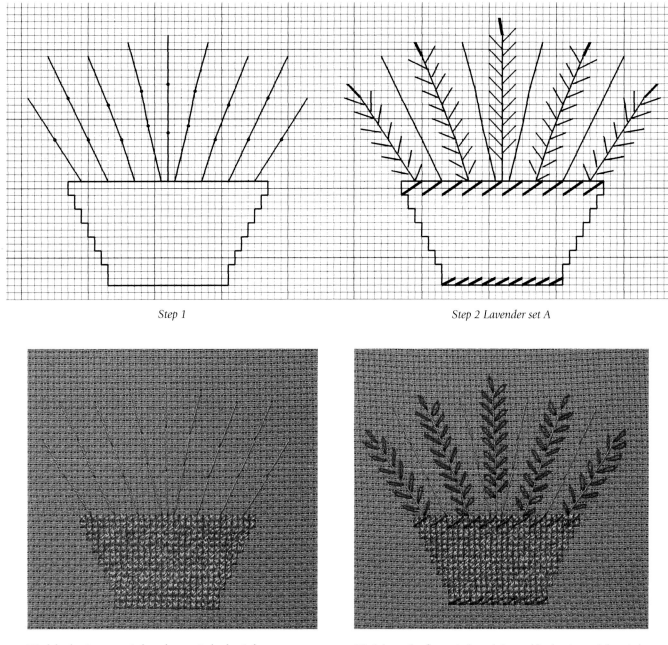

Step 1

Step 2 Lavender set A

Work basket in cross-stitch and stems in back-stitch.

Work lavender flower in lazy-daisy and basket in straight-stitch.

STEP 2
LAVENDER/SET A
Work in lazy-daisy stitch – it is easiest to work up one side of the stem and back down the other.
DMC 792 (1)
Basket edging – DMC 434 (1), DMC 433 (1) – straight-stitch, twist threads together.

STEP 3
LAVENDER/SET B
Work in lazy-daisy stitch:
Anchor 112 (1)
Basket – DMC 434 (1) – outline top edging in long back-stitch and begin diagonal pattern on basket – dots on graph indicate length of stitch.

STEP 4
FLOWER HEADS
Work rows of French-knots between the lavender petals:
Set A – Anchor 870 (1), Anchor 87 (2)
Set B – Anchor 870 (1), DMC 340 (2)
Basket – DMC 434 (1) – complete pattern

◆ Finally add some small white flowers to the arrangement.

WHITE FLOWERS
Anchor 300 (2) – French-knots in varying sizes – twist the thread and work some twice round the needle and others once.

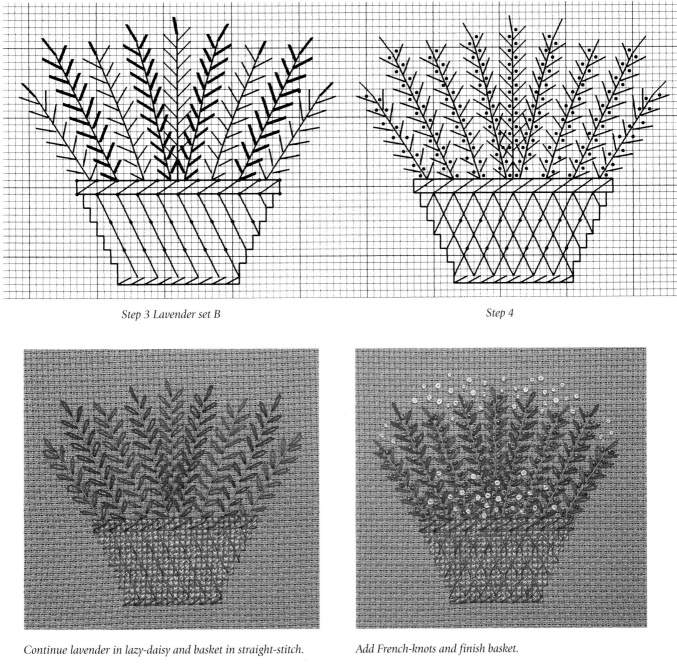

Step 3 Lavender set B

Step 4

Continue lavender in lazy-daisy and basket in straight-stitch.

Add French-knots and finish basket.

Sunflowers

In recent years the sunflower has become a favourite subject with many textile artists and has provided a wonderful opportunity for combining a dynamic pattern with a range of warm golden colours. As early as the seventeenth century, stylized motifs were appearing throughout Europe and in particular Germany, where a number of designs featured the decorative arrangement of the leaves as well as the flower. I thought that a jug of sunflowers would make an eye-catching centre-piece for a small sampler and could make an ideal gift to celebrate a number of occasions. I have placed the lettering in the form of a border and, by using a back-stitch to describe the capital letters, I have managed to include quite a lengthy piece of text, while at the same time making a neat and uniform edge to the design.

◆ Find the centre of the design and begin with the middle white flower.
◆ The amounts of threads for each colour combination are indicated in brackets (*see* page 20).
◆ The alphabet for this design is no. 7 (*see* page 121).

Materials Guide

◆ *See* 'Preparing to Work', page 18.
◆ Zweigart fabrics are quoted for all projects.

FABRICS
Lugana 25 count Pewter
Aida 14 count Summer Khaki
Fabric size approximately 12in sq. (31cm sq.)
Design size approximately 5½in sq. (15cm sq.)
Stitch count 74 × 74

THREADS
DMC and Anchor:
Green – DMC 320, 734, 3053, 3347
Yellow – DMC 725, 729, 782, 783
Brown – DMC 434, 3371
Blue – Anchor 162, 920, 921
White – DMC 3047, 3823

SUNFLOWERS

Work in cross-stitch:

Dark petals – DMC 729 (1), DMC 782 (1), DMC 434 (1)

Medium petals – DMC 782 (2), DMC 725(1)

Light petals – DMC 725 (1), DMC 729 (1), DMC 783 (1)

Brown centre – DMC 3371 (3)

Cream centre – DMC 3047 (3)

Stems – DMC 320 (1) – long back-stitch. Dots on graph represent length of stitch.

BORDER AND LETTERING

Work in back-stitch:

Border – DMC 782 (1)

Text – DMC 434 (1), DMC 782 (1)

Motif in corners – DMC 783 (1), DMC 725 (1)

WHITE DAISY

Work in cross-stitch:

Flower – DMC 3823 (2), DMC 3047 (1)

Centre – DMC 3371 (3)

LEAVES

Work in cross-stitch:

Light green – DMC 734 (1), DMC 3347 (1), DMC 3053 (1)

Dark green – DMC 320 (1), DMC 3347 (1), DMC 3053 (1)

JUG

Work in cross-stitch:

Light blue – Anchor 921 (2), Anchor 920 (1)

Dark blue – Anchor 162 (3)

Mother's Day

This is a fun little display of flowers that would make an ideal subject to celebrate any number of occasions. I have placed the brightly coloured stylized flowers in a large blue and white basket, using the text in the form of a border, and making a pattern with the arrangement of the words. I chose the theme of a present for mother, but first names and dates could just as easily be substituted and combined with different styles of lettering. Similarly, this simple design lends itself well to being interpreted in the same style of stitching used in the jug of tulips, and this could be achieved either by overworking the cross-stitch areas, or by outlining the flowers and leaves in back-stitch and filling in with a long satin-stitch. I have used this technique to depict the butterfly motifs, creating a wonderful silky sheen that adds a sparkle to the whole embroidery. The various options and possibilities for different colour schemes are endless and make this a most versatile composition.

Materials Guide

◆ *See* 'Preparing to Work', page 18.
◆ Zweigart fabrics are quoted for all projects.

FABRIC
Lugana 25 count Pewter
Aida 14 count Summer Khaki
Fabric size approximately 12in sq. (31cm sq.)
Design size approximately 6in sq. (16cm sq.)
Stitch count 78 × 78

THREADS
DMC and Anchor (+ denotes full skein):
Green – DMC 3012, 3347, Anchor 216, 217, 258
Yellow – DMC 743, 783
Orange – DMC 920, Anchor 316
Pink – Anchor 76
White – DMC 3047, 3823
Blue – Anchor 176 +

◆ Find centre of design and begin stitching middle leaf.
◆ The amounts of threads for each colour combination are indicated in brackets (*see* page 20).
◆ The alphabet for this design is no. 1 (*see* page 119).

BASKET
Work in cross-stitch:
Blue – Anchor 176 (3)
Cream – DMC 3047 (3)

LEAVES
Work in cross-stitch:
Light – DMC 3347 (2), DMC 3012 (1)
Medium – Anchor 258 (2), DMC 3012 (1)
Dark – Anchor 217 (2), Anchor 216 (1)

FLOWERS
Work in cross-stitch:
Pink – Anchor 76 (3)
Red – DMC 920 (2), Anchor 76 (1)
Orange – Anchor 316 (2), Anchor 76 (1)
Yellow – DMC 743 (2), DMC 783 (1)
Stems – Anchor 217 (1) – long back-stitch

BUTTERFLIES
Large White, *see* page 96.
Outline – DMC 743 (1) – back-stitch
Body – DMC 743 (2), DMC 783 (1) – cross-stitch
Wings – DMC 3823 (1) – long-stitch

LETTERING
Work in cross-stitch:
Blue – Anchor 176 (2)

Basket of Asters

THREADS
DMC and Anchor:
Brown – DMC 434, 680
Green – DMC 3347, Anchor 216
Yellow – DMC 743, 783
Orange – DMC 976, Anchor 316
Pink – Anchor 896, 76
Purple – DMC 333, 552

Materials Guide

◆ *See* 'Preparing to Work', page 18.
◆ Zweigart fabrics are quoted for all projects.

FABRIC
Aida 14 count Summer Khaki
Lugana 25 count Pewter
Design size approximately 3 × 2in (8 × 5.5cm)

Step 1 – This pretty little basket full of flowers is completely brought to life, when the cross-stitch base is reworked with a series of simple stitches.

Step 2

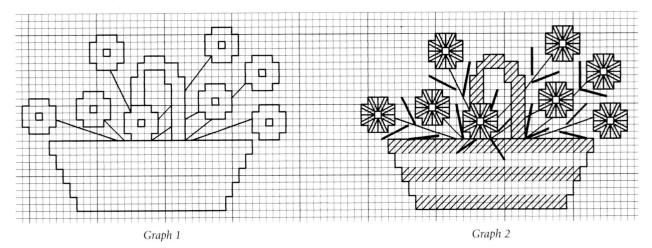

Graph 1   *Graph 2*

BASKET
Work the basket in cross-stitch – rework in satin stitch following pattern in Graph 2:
Base colour – DMC 434 (2)
Top-stitch – DMC 680 (1)

STEM
Anchor 216 (1) – long-stitch

LEAVES
Anchor 216 (1), DMC 3347 (1) – lazy-daisy

FLOWERS
Work the base and centre in cross-stitch – top-stitch in straight-stitch, following pattern in the Graph 2:
Orange base – DMC 976 (3)
   Centre – DMC 333 (3)
   Top-stitch – Anchor 316 (1)
Pink base – Anchor 896 (3)
   Centre – DMC 743 (3)
   Top-stitch – Anchor 76 (1)
Yellow base – DMC 783 (3)
   Centre – Anchor 896 (3)
   Top-stitch – DMC 743 (1)
Purple base – DMC 552 (3)
   Centre – DMC 783 (3)
   Top-stitch – DMC 333 (1)

Jug of Tulips

This jug of flowers is so easy to work and yet it gives the impression of being very complicated and skilful. The method of outlining the design in back-stitch and then filling-in with a long satin-stitch, was very popular during the early seventeenth and eighteenth centuries, particularly as it was a technique well suited for use on any type of fabric. English and European samplers of that period feature many examples of this style of embroidery, and the American tradition displays a highly original and creative use of this simple stitch. The actual technique is no more difficult than cross-stitch and in fact was probably the preferred method of working by young children, as it meant they were free from the constraints of making neat and even cross-stitches. Many designs at that time were drawn directly on to the cloth, and once the basic outline had been worked in back-stitch, all that remained was to fill in the motif with any number of random stitches. The use of long satin-stitches over an area creates a smooth flat surface that captures the light and gives a wonderful reflective quality to the overall design.

Materials Guide

◆ *See* 'Preparing to Work', page 18.
◆ Zweigart fabrics are quoted for all projects.

FABRIC
Lugana 25 count Pewter
Aida 14 count Summer Khaki
Design size 4 × 4¾in (11 × 12cm)
Stitch count 52 × 58

THREADS
DMC and Anchor:
Green – DMC 501, 502, 503, 3053
Yellow – DMC 729, 782, 3046
Pink – DMC 315, 316, 3727
Blue – Anchor 176
White – DMC 3823

◆ Find centre of design and begin stitching middle leaves.
◆ The amounts of threads in each colour combination are indicated in brackets (*see* page 20).

◆ This design could form the centrepiece for any of the projects illustrated on the previous pages or alternatively you might use it as part of your own composition for a commemorative sampler. The theme of your design will influence your choice of colours, and the sophisticated charm of these muted shades could be completely changed with a more lively and vibrant colour scheme.

STEP 1
1. Work the jug in cross-stitch and outline the leaves and flowers in long back-stitch (above graph) – the dots on the graph indicate the length of the stitches:

Jug – DMC 3823 (3)
Leaves/stems – DMC 501 (1)
Flowers:
    Yellow – DMC 782 (1)
    Pink – DMC 315 (1)

Step 1

Steps 2 and 3 are shown in progress, as the colours build up.

STEP 2

2. Fill in the outlined areas with a long satin-stitch (*see* graph below), spacing the stitches so that the fabric is just covered with the colour:

Leaves – DMC 502 (1)
Flowers:
    Yellow – DMC 729 (1)
    Pink – DMC 316 (1)

STEP 3

3. Continue in the same way, placing the second colour in between the first set of stitches so as to build up a rich surface texture:
Leaves:
    DMC 503 (1)
    DMC 3053 (1) – finally place this colour sparingly on top of each leaf, to give an added highlight
Flowers:
    Yellow DMC 3046 (1)
    Pink DMC 3727 (1)

JUG
DMC 3823 (1) – rework the handle and rim with a diagonal satin-stitch to disguise the squareness of the cross-stitch.
Anchor 176 (1) – following the dark lines on the graph, outline the rim, handle, and base in back-stitch.
Anchor 176 (1) – work pattern on jug in long back-stitch.

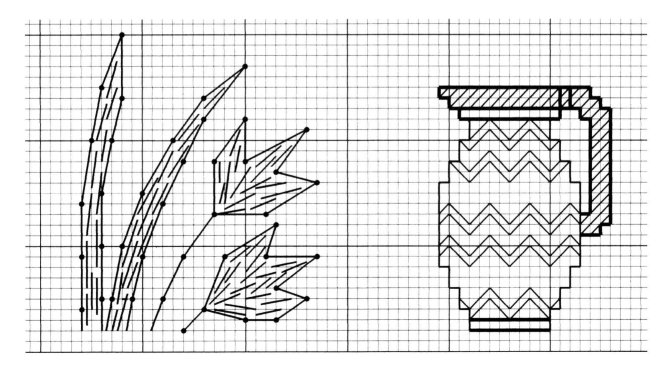

3 Country House

The fascination with depicting buildings in embroidery had lead to it becoming the most popular choice of subject by the mid-eighteenth century, and samplers across Europe and America reflect this interest with an amazing diversity of styles and originality. Very few examples appear to be portraits of actual buildings, but were in the main a series of designs which were copied from an array of standard patterns. The selection available in any one school would probably have been quite limited, and yet the scope and singular quality of each individual interpretation is astonishing.

The majority of buildings were worked in a range of naturalistic colours, perhaps in some cases even reflecting the local building materials, such as brick, stone or granite. It is interesting to note that a number of examples, from particular areas and regions, all seem to have the same architectural styles and colour schemes. Occasionally, more imaginative and fanciful interpretations can be found, although usually only from certain American schools, where a number of bright, primary colours have been used to illustrate the buildings, giving the embroidery an intrinsic charm of its own. Cross-stitch worked in the form of petit point was the most commonly used technique, as the smaller scale of stitches allowed for the addition of details, such as brick bonding patterns and roof tiles, to be incorporated into the design.

OPPOSITE: The traditional house and garden sampler is still a subject that appeals to many embroiderers, and this basic design could be adapted in a number of ways. For instance, a row of figures, representing family members, would fit into the area immediately below the house, in place of the strip border and lettering. Also the main cross-stitch border is very easy to extend and any names and dates could be added at the base.

Materials Guide

◆ *See* 'Preparing to Work', page 18.
◆ Zweigart fabrics are quoted for all projects.

FABRIC
Lugana 25 count Natural or Pewter
    Fabric size 19¾ × 23in (50 × 59cm)
    Design size 11½ × 15in (29 × 38cm)
    Stitch count 143 × 191
Aida 14 count Barn Grey
    Fabric size 18¾ × 22in (47.5 × 56.5cm)
    Design size 10½ × 14in (27 × 35.5cm)
    Stitch count 143 × 191

THREADS
DMC and Anchor (+ denotes full skein):
Green – DMC 500 +, 3013, 3347, Anchor 216 +, 859 +, 879 +
Blue/Purple – DMC 333, 3810, Anchor 169
Brown – DMC 434, 611, 612 +, 3371, Anchor 373, 904
Yellow – DMC 680, 729 +, 782 +, 783, 3820
Red/Pink – DMC 356 +, 3721 +, Anchor 936 +
White/Beige – DMC 613 +, Anchor 386 +
Grey – DMC 414 +, 415, 535 +

◆ Mark in guide-lines as described on page 19.
◆ Count up and place in small border below house. Begin with right tree.
◆ The amounts of threads for each colour combination are indicated in brackets (*see* page 20).
◆ The alphabet for this design is no. 2 (*see* page 119).

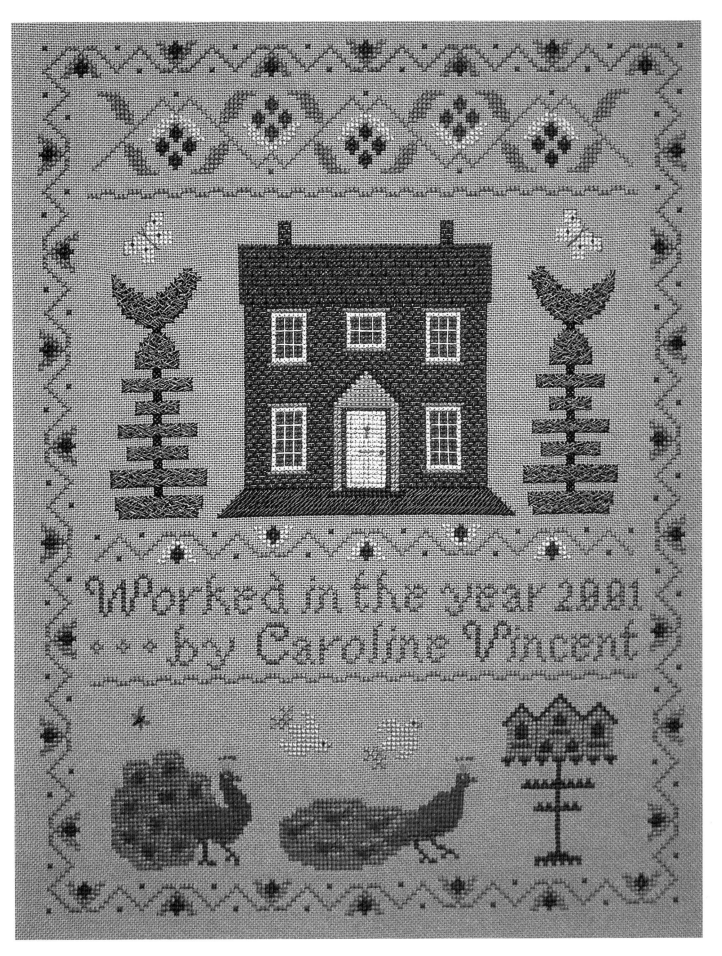

Step 1   *Step 2*   *Step 3*   *Step 4*

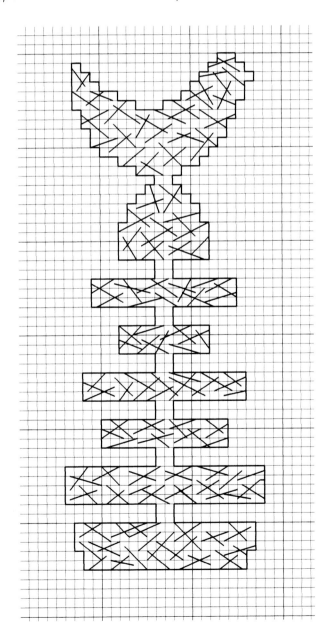

Topiary Trees

This is a very simple way of creating a rich surface of colour and texture, which gives added character to the formal outline of the topiary trees.

Work the base colour for the trees in cross-stitch and build up the three layers of colours using a random long-stitch. The pattern for the stitches on the graph are only a guide and need not be followed accurately, as this style of work relies on an individual interpretation. Once, the first set of stitches is in place, continue with the other colours in the same way, filling in any obvious gaps at the end. If possible, try to set aside a period of time to work the overstitching, as you will find you get into a rhythm and pattern of working and it is much quicker and easier to complete.

TREES
1. DMC 500 (2) – cross-stitch
2. DMC 3013 (1) – long-stitch
3. DMC 3347 (1) – long-stitch
4. Anchor 216 (1) – long-stitch

◆ However, if you preferred to work the trees as cross-stitch motifs, a combination of the above colours will create an interesting mottled effect that adds character to the design. The three threads need to be twisted together as you work, to get the maximum variation in the colours.

Cross-stitch trees – DMC 500 (1), DMC 3347 (1),
   Anchor 216 (1) twist

BUTTERFLIES
Small White, *see* page 97.

Details of House, Porch and Borders

House Details

The bonding pattern on the bricks is made with back-stitch, working over two stitches in a horizontal direction and up one stitch in a vertical direction. I find it easiest to begin stitching in the top right-hand corner of the building and to work back down, across the design. The roof tiles are worked in the same way, only the pattern is larger, travelling over three stitches horizontally and two stitches vertically. Each glazing bar on the windows is worked as one long straight-stitch. Keep the threads slightly twisted together to stop them from separating.

Brick pattern – Anchor 373 (1) – back-stitch
Roof tiles – DMC 535 (1) – back-stitch
Window bars – Anchor 386 (2) – straight-stitch

Borders

Work in cross-stitch.
Top border:
    Beige stems and leaves – DMC 612 (2)
    White flowers – DMC 613 (2), Anchor 386 (1)
    Purple flowers/spot – DMC 333 (1),
       DMC 3721 (1), DMC 611 (1)
    Blue flowers/spot – DMC 3810 (1), DMC 333 (1),
       DMC 611 (1)
Middle border:
    Beige – DMC 612 (2)
    White – DMC 613 (2), Anchor 386 (1)
    Pink – DMC 356 (1), DMC 3721 (1),
       Anchor 936 (1)

Porch Details

I have added some details to the front door, so as to disguise the harsh and rather dominating effect of a completely white space, and have overstitched the surrounding stone-work to give the porch more definition and interest.

Work the panels for the door in normal back-stitch. Twist the threads for the letter-box and knocker. Work the door-knob as double French-knot.

The patterns on the columns and porch roof are worked in a long straight-stitch, with the threads twisted a number of times to create a twill effect.

Door panels – DMC 612 (1) – back-stitch
Door-knob – DMC 782 (3) – French-knot
Letter-box – DMC 782 (3) – straight-stitch
Knocker – DMC 782 (3) – French knot – straight-
    stitch
Porch roof and columns – DMC 613 (2) – straight-
    stitch – twist

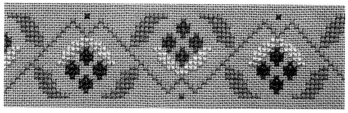

Top border

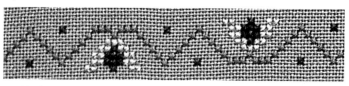

Middle border

House

The different scale of the patterns on the bricks and roof tiles helps to create a more interesting and varied surface texture that completely transforms the appearance of the building. The natural colour of bricks can vary enormously, and any number of combinations of brown and red tones could be used to make a particular shade, but remember that the overall colour will become much lighter once it has been overstitched with the bonding pattern. On this occasion I have chosen quite a deep reddish/pink to depict the building, as I felt that these colours were more suited to the theme of the composition.

◆ Begin by working all the house and grass area in cross-stitch; then add the details (*see* opposite page).

HOUSE
Work in cross-stitch:
Brickwork – DMC 356 (1), DMC 3721 (1),
    Anchor 936 (1)
Window frame – Anchor 386 (3)
Lintel and sill – DMC 612 (3)
Window panes – DMC 414 (3)
Porch stonework – DMC 613 (2), DMC 612 (1)
Porch steps and roof – Anchor 904 (3)

Door – Anchor 386 (2), DMC 613 (1)
Roof/house – DMC 535 (2), DMC 414 (1)

GRASS
Work base in cross-stitch and rework in slanting-stitch (*see* page 85):
Base – Anchor 879 (2)
Top-stitch – Anchor 216 (1)

Detail of house in base colours.

Peacocks and Dovecotes

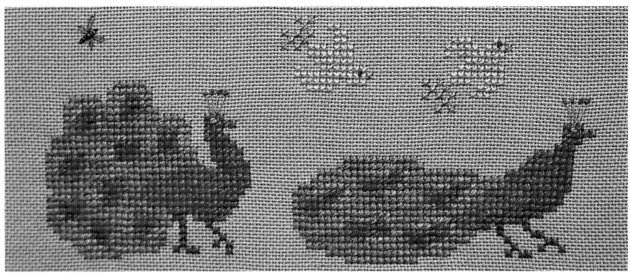

This display of peacocks in a garden setting makes a very effective statement along the base of the embroidery, with the two classic poses showing the tail open in pride and the other in the closed position, trailing on the ground. I have used quite a vibrant mix of colours to do justice to the wonderful array of feathers and I have re-used some of the shades in the stylized border, at the top of the design. Work the peacocks in cross-stitch, matching the symbols on the graph to the colours.

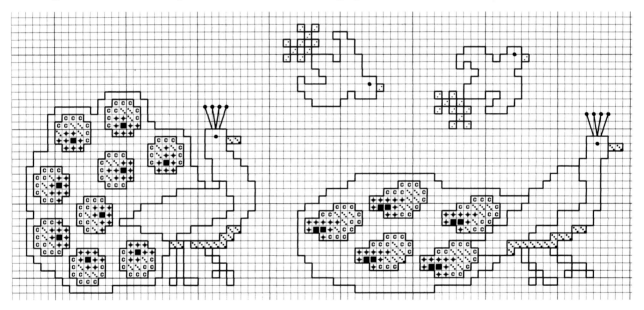

PEACOCK TAIL
Green – Anchor 216 (1), Anchor 859 (1),
   DMC 3810 (1)
c – DMC 3820 (2), DMC 782 (1)
+ – Anchor 169 (2), DMC 3810 (1)
■ – DMC 333 (3)
·.■ – DMC 782 (2), DMC 434 (1)

PEACOCK BODY
Blue – Anchor 169 (2), DMC 3810 (1)
Purple – DMC 333 (2), DMC 3810 (1)
Yellow – DMC 782 (2), DMC 434 (1)
Legs – Anchor 904 (2), DMC 434 (1)
Beak – DMC 782 (2), DMC 434 (1)

CROWN
Yellow – DMC 729 (1) – long-stitch
Blue – DMC 3810 (1), Anchor 169 (1) – French-knot
Eye – DMC 3820 (2), DMC 729 (1) – French-knot

DOVES
Work in cross-stitch:
Body – DMC 415 (2)
Tail – DMC 414 (1), DMC 415 (1)
Beak – DMC 414 (1)
Eye – DMC 3721 (1), Anchor 936 (1) – French-knot

BEE
See page 95.

Peacocks

At one time no country house would have been complete without a parade of peacocks, strutting around the lawns. During the Tudor period they were regarded as royal birds, and were kept for their attributes in gracing a banqueting table as much as for decoration in the gardens. It is of no surprise then, that they should feature so frequently in many of the earliest surviving English samplers, and were often worked in a very naturalistic manner, which suggests that they were probably copies from illustrations. However, as the trend towards the singular use of cross-stitch increased, patterns were modified and simplified resulting in a number of highly stylized and geometric designs, which were to become one of the favourite schoolroom motifs during the nineteenth century.

There seem to be very few examples of peacocks in American samplers, and they are rarely included with the assortment of other animals that are arranged in such a random manner on the expansive green lawns. However, there are some particularly interesting patterns in many early German and Dutch samplers, where a number of striking poses have been combined with some very original colour schemes, including the use of a series of muted browns and greens to illustrate the tail feathers. Several examples show a very complex tail arrangement, made up of numerous 'eye' motifs and portrayed in a range of subtle blues and greens. The scale and intricacy of the motifs varies considerably, and some of the smaller designs even featured in border patterns.

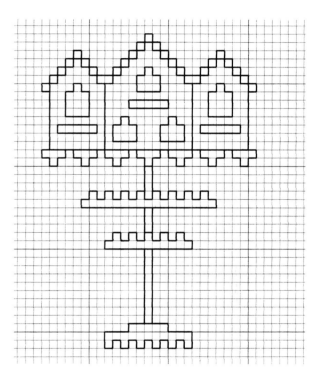

Dovecote for the Country House project.

DOVECOTE
Work in cross-stitch – outline roof in back-stitch:
Roof and perches – DMC 356 (1), DMC 3721 (1),
  Anchor 936 (1)
Walls of cote – DMC 729 (2), DMC 782 (1)
Openings and pole – Anchor 904 (3)
Roof outline and division of cote – Anchor 904 (1) –
  back-stitch

LETTERING
Work in cross-stitch:
Text – DMC 612 (1), DMC 611 (1)
Capitals – DMC 611 (2)

BORDERS
Outer edge and yellow band:
Yellow – DMC 729 (2), DMC 782 (1)
Green – Anchor 216 (1), Anchor 859 (1)
Pink – DMC 356 (1), DMC 3721 (1), Anchor 936 (1)

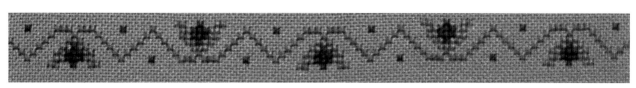

Outer border

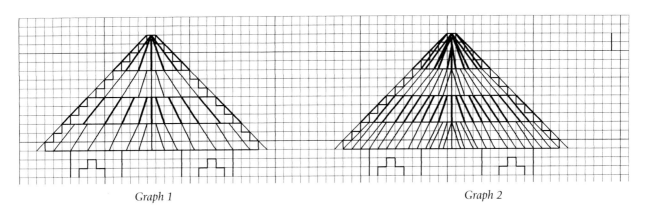

Graph 1   *Graph 2*

DOVECOTE THATCH ROOF (*see also* page 47)
STEP 1
Rework the cross-stitch bands on the roof using a long-stitch.

Following the pattern of lines in Graph 1, work the first set of stitches.
Light yellow – DMC 729 (1)
Dark yellow – DMC 680 (1)

STEP 2
Continue in the same way placing the second set of stitches between the first, to build up the surface texture. Follow pattern in Graph 2.
Light yellow – DMC 676 (1)
Dark yellow – DMC 729 (1)

Base colours in cross-stitch.

Detail of completed thatch.

DOVES
Work in cross-stitch:
Body – DMC 415 (2)
Tail – DMC 414 (1),
    DMC 415 (1)
Beak – DMC 414 (1) –
    straight-stitch
Eye – DMC 221 (1) –
    French-knot

◆ The method of building up the colours and surface texture to resemble the quality of the straw, would work very well on the style of roof on dovecote B, where a vertical straight stitch could be used to form three or four rows of thatch.

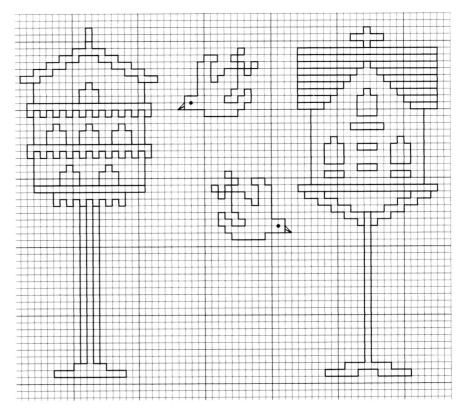

Alternative Dovecotes

Dovecotes first appeared in England after the Norman invasion, when thousands of large barn-like structures were built for the sole purpose of breeding pigeons, as an economical source of food. Gradually the need for such intensive farming was reduced to a more domestic scale, and the idea of rearing the birds as a leisure activity was established. By the eighteenth century, it became very fashionable for all the large country estates to include an ornate brick dove-house as a decorative architectural feature in the grounds, while the charming miniature wooden cots balanced on thin poles became commonplace in the garden.

It was during this period that the dovecote motif first began to appear in samplers and became a very popular subject in Dutch and German embroideries with an array of patterns for elaborate, decorative buildings, which were quite often the focal point of the design. The dovecote motif was a more modest affair in English samplers and was usually portrayed as a simple garden structure. Conversely, I have found very few examples in American needlework, apart from the samplers originating from New Hampshire, where a design for a farmhouse, alongside a barn and dovecote, featured as one of the standard patterns during the nineteenth century.

Dovecote A   Dovecote B

The dovecote motif makes an ideal subject to form the central theme of a small embroidery, and would look equally at home surrounded by ducks and hens as it would amongst the playful hares of the woodland scene. There are numerous possibilities for varying the colour schemes and individual style of these buildings, which can easily be adapted to suit a particular design.

Yellow – DMC 782 (1), DMC 783 (1), DMC 729 (1)
Blue – DMC 3810 (2), Anchor 922 (1)
Dark brown – DMC 3371 (1), Anchor 905 (1)

DOVECOTE B
Work in cross-stitch:
White – DMC 612 (1), DMC 613 (1), DMC 3823 (1)
Light red – DMC 356 (1), DMC 434 (1), DMC 612 (1)
Dark red – DMC 355 (2), DMC 434 (1)
Brown – DMC 610 (2), Anchor 905 (1)
Green – Anchor 216 (2), DMC 3347 (1)

DOVECOTE A
Work in cross-stitch:
Brown – DMC 434 (1), DMC 801 (1), DMC 611 (1)

DOVECOTE
Stand – Anchor 921 (3)
Cote C – Anchor 920 (3)
Cote D – Anchor 921 (2), Anchor 920 (1)
Doors – Anchor 922 (3)
Roof A – DMC 729 (3)
Roof B – DMC 680 (3)

THATCH ROOF
For details *see* page 44.

DOVES
Left dove / stitch direction
Right dove \ stitch direction
Body – DMC 648 (3)
Wings – DMC 648 (2), DMC 646 (1)
Tail/Beak – DMC 646 (3)
Eye – DMC 3802 (2) – French-knot

LETTERING
DMC 646 (2)

RABBITS
Left rabbit \ stitch direction
Right rabbit / stitch direction
Brown – DMC 801 (2), DMC 434 (1)
White – DMC 613 (2), DMC 3823 (1)
Eye – DMC 310 (3)
Leaf – DMC 3052 (1), DMC 3053 (1) – lazy-daisy
Stem – DMC 3051 (1) – straight-stitch
Flower – DMC 3722 (1), DMC 3802 (1),
    Anchor 895 (1) – French-knot

URN
Dark blue – Anchor 922 (3)
Medium blue – Anchor 921 (3)
Light blue – Anchor 920 (3)
White – DMC 613 (3)

BORDERS
Pink – DMC 3722 (1), Anchor 895 (1)
Green – DMC 3052 (2)
Yellow – DMC 725 (2)

This pretty garden scene makes an ideal subject to commemorate a number of occasions. The design is mainly worked in cross-stitch, but is much enhanced by the addition of some textural detail to the dovecote roof and the hollyhock flowers.

Dovecote and Rabbits

Materials Guide

FABRIC
Aida 14 count Antique
Lugana 25 count beige
    Fabric size 10 × 10in (26 × 26cm)
    Design size 7 × 7in (18.5 × 18.5cm)
    Stitch count 99 × 99

THREADS
DMC and Anchor (+ denotes full skein):
Green – DMC 3051, 3052, 3053
Yellow – DMC 676, 680, 725, 729
Brown – DMC 434, 801
Blue – Anchor 920, 921 +, 922
Red/Pink – DMC 3722 +, 3802, Anchor 895 +
White – DMC 613, 3823
Black/Grey – DMC 310, 646, 648

◆ The alphabet for this design is no. 7 (*see* page 121).
◆ Work the whole design in cross-stitch, and then rework details.
◆ Change the direction of the stitches on the rabbits and doves

FLOWERS
Dark – DMC 3802 (3)
Medium – DMC 3722 (3)
Light – Anchor 895 (3)
Centres – DMC 725 (3) – double cross-stitch
Leaves – DMC 3052 (2), DMC 3051 (1)
Stems – DMC 3053 (2), DMC 3052 (1)

FLOWERS TOP-STITCH
Work a straight-stitch following the pattern on the left-hand graph and using a single thread in the same colour.

Pattern for overstitching on the flowers.

4 Farmyard Animals

Small domestic livestock in the form of ducks and hens are a particular feature of many European samplers from the eighteenth century. Farm animals during this period were considered a valuable asset, often housed within the farmstead and left free to roam indoors, much like pets. It is no surprise then, that a large and resplendent cockerel was a common motif in so many German samplers, and it would be nice to think that it represented a prized specimen, besides probably having some symbolic or heraldic meaning. Perhaps this pride in poultry keeping travelled with the settlers to America, as there are numerous examples of expansive green lawns covered with various displays of hens, geese and cockerels.

This is a fun design, including rows of little farm animals, an apple orchard and a traditional-style alphabet. The colours of the Gloucestershire Old Spots, alongside the Embden and Greylag geese are a perfect complement to the soft earthy colours of the hens. The various patterns of the Silver Spangled Hamburgh, Marsh Daisy, Brown Leghorn and Scots Grey cockerel, disguise the fact that these motifs are basically worked in a cross-stitch, and the techniques involved in creating the various markings are all very simple. The use of satin-stitch on the beehive creates a wonderful creamy colour, and transforms the cross-stitch with a rich textural surface.

OPPOSITE: Stories and pictures of farm animals are always firm favourites with children and this sampler of little pigs, geese and hens makes an ideal design to commemorate a birth or christening. With this in mind, I have designed the woodland sampler to exactly the same dimensions, so that the pair of embroideries could be used for two children in the same family.

Materials Guide

◆ *See* 'Preparing to Work', page 18.
◆ Zweigart fabrics are quoted for all projects.

FABRIC
Lugana 25 count Pewter
   Fabric size 19½ × 23in (49.5 × 59cm)
   Design size 11½ × 15in (29 × 38cm)
   Stitch count 145 × 193
Aida 14 count Summer Khaki
   Fabric size 18¾ × 22in (47.5 × 56.5cm)
   Design size 10½ × 14in (27 × 36cm)
   Stitch count 145 × 193

THREADS
DMC and Anchor (+ denotes full skein):
Green – DMC 470, 502 ++, 503 ++, 3012,
   Anchor 859 +
Brown – DMC 434, 610, 612 +, 3371,
   Anchor 392, 393 +, 905
Blue – Anchor 410, 920 +, 921 +
Yellow – DMC 676, 729 +, 782 +, 783
Red/pink – DMC 316 +, 400, 3726 +, Anchor 13
White – DMC 613 +, 746, Anchor 386 ++
Black/Grey – DMC 646, 647

◆ Mark in guide-lines as described on page 19.
◆ Count up to narrow border under pig and begin here.
◆ The amounts of threads for each colour combination are indicated in brackets (*see* page 20).
◆ The alphabet for this design is no. 3 (*see* page 120).

Scots Grey Cockerel

This magnificent cockerel, with its uniform pattern and striking tail feathers, has always been a particular favourite with artists and illustrators in every field of design. I decided that I just had to find a way of recreating this wonderful example of a rooster through embroidery, and after puzzling over the problem for a while, I was surprised to discover such a simple solution. By working through two basic stages, comprising of a cross-stitch base, which is then reworked in back-stitch to form the markings, the whole effect can be achieved very quickly and easily. The mottled texture of the base colours helps to give the motif a more natural appearance, and by using a very dark brown, rather than a black colour to outline the distinctive patterning, the strength of the contrasting tones is subdued and softened.

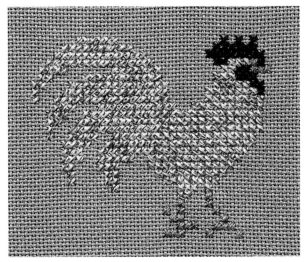

Step 1

1. Following the graph opposite, work the base colours in cross-stitch, changing the direction of the top stitch on the tail and body.
   Tail – / stitch direction
   Body – \ stitch direction
   Twist the threads every so often to mix the colours.
   Cockerel:
   Base – DMC 746 (2), Anchor 393 (1) – twist
   Feet – DMC 729 (2), Anchor 393 (1)
   Comb – Anchor 13 (2), DMC 400 (1)
   Beak – DMC 783 (3)
2. Rework base in back-stitch, using a single thread. The dots on the graph indicate the length of each stitch.
   Top-stitch – DMC 3371 (1)
   Eye – DMC 3371 (3) – French-knot

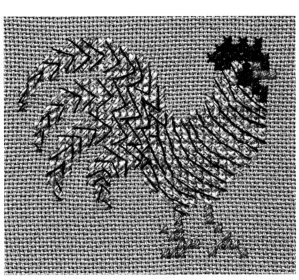

Step 2

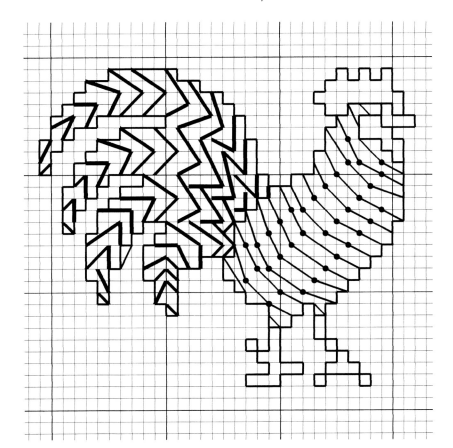

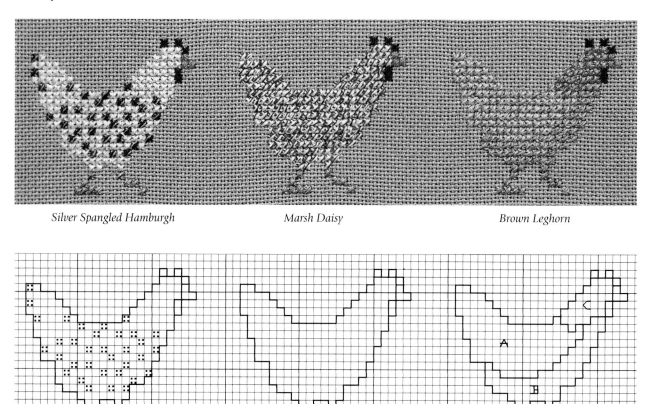

Silver Spangled Hamburgh   Marsh Daisy   Brown Leghorn

Graph 1   Graph 2   Graph 3

Hens

Chickens are such fascinating and intriguing creatures, and the enormous diversity of patterns and colours amongst the breeds provides a wealth of information for the embroiderer to work from. Their very names conjure up images of textures, colours and atmosphere, with many breeds being named after their place of origin: Speckled Sussex, Plymouth Rock, Rhode Island Red, Black Minorca and Marsh Daisy are just a few of the varieties that have inspired me to try and find a way of depicting their characteristic differences, through stitches. And, in fact, I discovered a very simple technique that made it possible to recreate the speckled textural effects of the feathers and make endless subtle variations to the colour combinations.

◆ Work the base colours for the hens in cross-stitch following the graph patterns above. In some of the patterns the threads will need to be twisted together to create a more random and varied effect with the colour. Simply hold the needle up and turn it a couple of times to twist the threads together. You will probably need to repeat this action every so often, as you continue working.

GRAPH 1
SILVER SPANGLED HAMBURGH
Base/white – Anchor 386 (2), DMC 613 (1)
Dark spots – Anchor 905 (2), Anchor 392 (1) – twist

GRAPH 2
MARSH DAISY
Base – Anchor 386 (2), DMC 434 (1) – twist

GRAPH 3
BROWN LEGHORN
A. Base – DMC 613 (2), DMC 612 (1)
B. Base – DMC 612 (2), DMC 613 (1)
C. Base – DMC 729 (2), DMC 782 (1)

DETAILS
These are the same for each hen and are worked in cross-stitch:
Feet – DMC 729 (2), Anchor 393 (1)
Comb – Anchor 13 (3)
Beak – DMC 783 (3)
Eye – DMC 3371 (3) – French-knot

I have kept the same basic shape for all the hens in this design, as I like the idea of using the motifs to make a repetitive pattern in the composition, whilst still being able to make each individual hen appear different through the use of colour and implied textures. The hens from my Mill Farm sampler are also the same size, and you could substitute any of these varieties quite easily if you preferred. Alternatively these sets of colours could be exchanged with the patterns and shapes of the hens in the hen-house design. There are many other breeds that you may want to include in an embroidery, either for their particular colour or perhaps for personal reasons, and you could easily adapt this basic technique to plan your own designs.

◆ Rework the hens using a half cross-stitch angled in the direction indicated on the graph. Twist the threads where indicated. I have added a few flecks of very pale beige to the body of the Silver Hamburgh to soften the colour change between the head and tail end. These are indicated on the graph by the symbols in the squares, but you could place them at random as you work, adding a few more in a slightly darker colour if you wish.

GRAPH 4
SILVER SPANGLED HAMBURGH
Head top-stitch – Anchor 393 (1), DMC 3371 (1) – twist
Body top-stitch – Anchor 392 (1)

GRAPH 5
MARSH DAISY
Top-stitch – DMC 400 (1), DMC 729 (1) – twist

GRAPH 6
BROWN LEGHORN
A. Top-stitch – DMC 434 (1), DMC 610 (1) – twist
C. Top-stitch – DMC 3371 (1)

CHICK
Work in cross-stitch:
Body – DMC 612 (1), DMC 676 (1)
Feet and Beak – DMC 729 (2), DMC 612 (1)
Eye – DMC 3371 (2) – French-knot

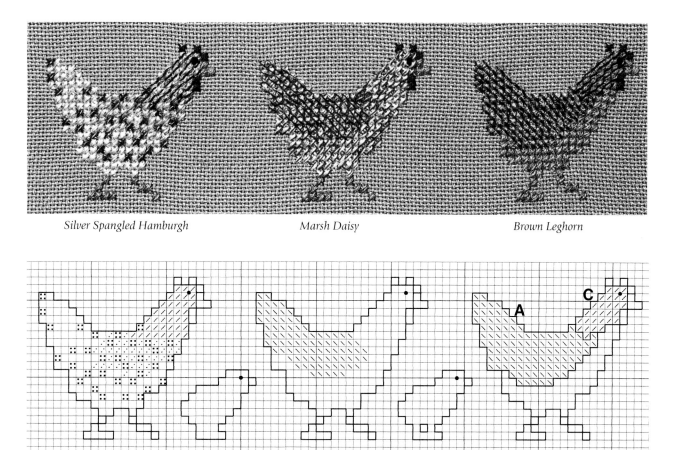

Silver Spangled Hamburgh   *Marsh Daisy*   *Brown Leghorn*

Graph 4   *Graph 5*   *Graph 6*

Gloucester Old Spot

There appear to be virtually no examples of the domestic pig in any early samplers, and it was not until the late twentieth century that this engaging little animal came into its own – mainly owing to its success as a character in children's literature. The exaggerated tones of pink that always accompany any stylized illustrations make this motif an ideal subject for providing the opportunity to include a colour that is usually only associated with designs and patterns of flowers. In this instance I have used quite a bright pink, from the blue end of the spectrum, and combined it with a pale brown to create a more muted shade. Whereas in the example featured on page 55 I used a more red-pink, as it was better suited to the overall colour scheme in the embroidery.

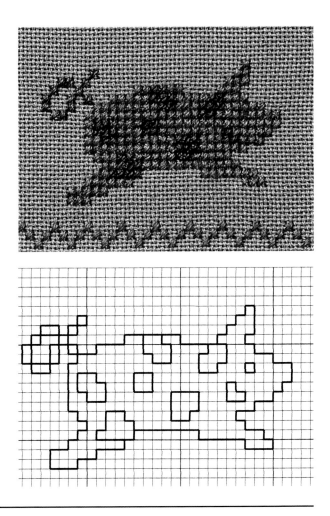

PIGS
Work in cross-stitch:
Pink body – DMC 316 (2), Anchor 392 (1)
Brown spots – Anchor 393 (2), Anchor 905 (1)
Tail – DMC 316 (2), DMC 3726 (1)
Eye – Anchor 410 (3) – cross-stitch

Tree No. 1   Tree No. 2

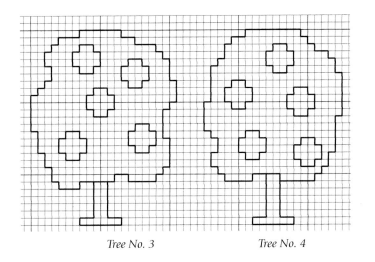

Tree No. 3   Tree No. 4

Apple Trees

◆ The patterns for trees 1 and 2 are on page 50.

TREES
Work in cross-stitch:
1. DMC 470 (1), Anchor 859 (1), DMC 503 (1)
2. DMC 502 (1), DMC 503 (1), DMC 3012 (1)
3. DMC 3012 (1), DMC 470 (1), DMC 503 (1)
4. DMC 502 (1), DMC 503 (1), Anchor 859 (1)
Red apples – DMC 3726 (2), DMC 400 (1)
Tree trunks – Anchor 393 (2), DMC 434 (1)

BORDERS AND ALPHABETS
Work in cross-stitch:
Borders:
    Blue – Anchor 921 (2), Anchor 920 (1)
    Pink – DMC 316 (2), DMC 3726 (1)
    White – Anchor 386 (3)
    Green – Anchor 859 (3)
Alphabets:
    Green – Anchor 859 (2), DMC 502 (1)
    Pink – DMC 316 (2), DMC 3726 (1)
    Yellow – DMC 729 (1), DMC 782 (1), DMC 612 (1)

Ducks and Geese

A variety of motifs depicting farmyard ducks and geese feature in many early European samplers, and at a later date became a popular subject in American embroideries. The bird was nearly always portrayed as a flat area of colour using a basic cross-stitch, and quite often it is difficult to decide whether the motif is that of a duck or goose, as the similar characteristics of the long neck and snowy white colouring make it easy to confuse the two breeds. When I decided to include some ducks in the Mill Farm embroidery, I thought that it would be fun to try and suggest the smooth surface of the fine velvety feathers. I first worked the motif in cross-stitch using an off-white colour, such as DMC 746, and then overstitched the area with a slanting-stitch in the same colour, which gave the impression of the silky coat and also disguised the pronounced squareness of the cross-stitch. In the farmyard project featured here, I decided to make the birds look more like geese and also to create a different sort of surface texture by mixing the shades of thread and changing the direction of the stitches. This first example resembles the all-white Embden goose, and by adding a further set of stitches to the same motif, it was possible to depict the distinctive patterns of the Greylag goose.

BEES
See page 95.

BEEHIVE
See page 65.

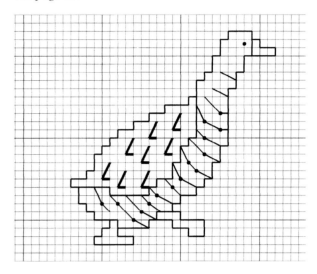

Graph for both geese.

Following the colours for the Embden Goose, work both the geese in cross-stitch, changing the directions of the top stitch, on the body and wing.

◆ Stitch direction on body \
◆ Stitch direction on wing /

EMBDEN GOOSE
Body – Anchor 386 (2), DMC 613 (1)
Wing – Anchor 386 (2), DMC 612 (1)
Feet/beak – DMC 783 (2),
    DMC 3726 (1)
Eye – DMC 3371 (3) – French-knot

GREYLAG GOOSE
Body – Anchor 393 (1)
Wing – DMC 610 (1)

◆ Rework the second goose with back-stitch, following the pattern on the graph. The dots on the body represent the length of the stitch.

Embden goose and Greylag goose.

The ducks and pigs from the Mill Farm sampler were reworked in slanting-stitch.

Mill Farm Hens

◆ Work the base colours for the three hens in cross-stitch, graph 1. Then overstitch all three with a half cross-stitch, following the patterns on Graphs 2 and 3.

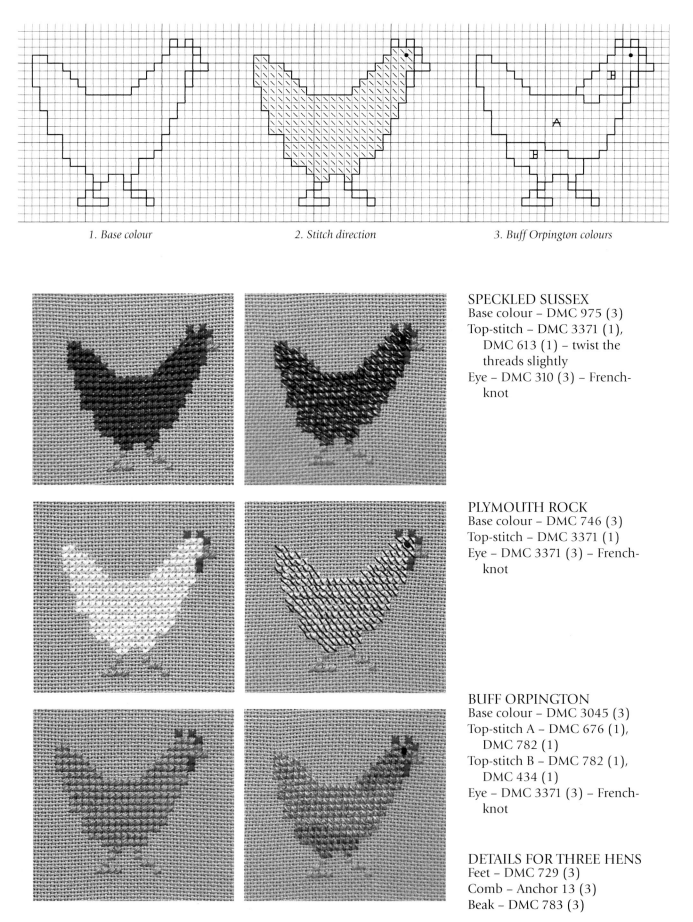

1. Base colour   *2. Stitch direction*   *3. Buff Orpington colours*

SPECKLED SUSSEX
Base colour – DMC 975 (3)
Top-stitch – DMC 3371 (1),
    DMC 613 (1) – twist the
    threads slightly
Eye – DMC 310 (3) – French-
    knot

PLYMOUTH ROCK
Base colour – DMC 746 (3)
Top-stitch – DMC 3371 (1)
Eye – DMC 3371 (3) – French-
    knot

BUFF ORPINGTON
Base colour – DMC 3045 (3)
Top-stitch A – DMC 676 (1),
    DMC 782 (1)
Top-stitch B – DMC 782 (1),
    DMC 434 (1)
Eye – DMC 3371 (3) – French-
    knot

DETAILS FOR THREE HENS
Feet – DMC 729 (3)
Comb – Anchor 13 (3)
Beak – DMC 783 (3)

A lively little design full of bright colours and movement, with the cockerel scuffing up the straw as he runs along.

Hen House

Materials Guide

◆ *See* 'Preparing to Work', page 18.
◆ Zweigart fabrics are quoted for all projects.

FABRIC
Aida 14 count Summer Khaki
Lugana 25 count Pewter
Fabric size approximately 12½ × 15in (32 × 39cm)
Design size approximately 7 × 9in (19 × 24cm)
Stitch count 97 × 125

THREADS
DMC and Anchor (+ denotes full skein):
Green – DMC 320 +, 500, 501, 522 +,
    Anchor 189, 227
Brown – DMC 434, 611, 612, 3371, Anchor 905
Blue – DMC 796, Anchor 410, 920 +, 921 +
Yellow – DMC 676, 725, 729, 782, 783
Red/pink – DMC 400, 920, 3722, Anchor 13
White – DMC 613, 3823
Black/grey – DMC 310, Anchor 401

◆ Find the centre of the design and begin with ramp of hen house.
◆ The amounts of threads for each colour combination are indicated in brackets (*see* page 20).
◆ The alphabet for this design is no. 6 (*see* page 121).

LETTERING
DMC 611 (1)

BORDERS
Work in cross-stitch:
Top:
    Yellow – DMC 783 (2), DMC 729 (1)
    Orange – DMC 920 (2), DMC 434 (1)
    Green – DMC 522 (2), DMC 320 (1)

Bottom:
    Pink – DMC 3722 (2)
    Green – DMC 522 (2), DMC 320 (1)
    Brown – DMC 434 (2)
Middle:
    Green – DMC 522 (2), DMC 320 (1)

58

HEN HOUSE

Work the little hutch in cross-stitch using two shades of blue, which are then separated with a dark blue line of back-stitch:

Dark blue – Anchor 921 (2), Anchor 920 (1)
Light blue – Anchor 920 (3)
Blue back-stitch lines – DMC 796 (1)
Red – DMC 920 (2), DMC 434 (1)
Yellow – DMC 729 (3)
Brown in door and window – Anchor 905 (2), DMC 611 (1)
Ramp – DMC 611 (3)
Lines on ramp – Anchor 905 (1) – long-stitch
Window bars – DMC 729 (2) – twist

BUTTERFLIES

Brimstone Yellow and Orange Tip, *see* page 96.

GRASS

Work in long-stitch:
Green – DMC 320 (1), Anchor 227 (1)
Flowers – DMC 3722 (3) – French-knot

STRAW

Work three colours separately:
Dark lines – DMC 434 (1)
Light lines – DMC 676 (1) and DMC 729 (1)

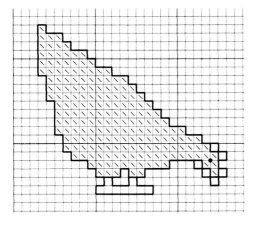

Black Ancona Step 1   *Step 2*

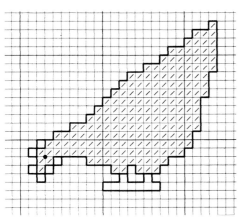
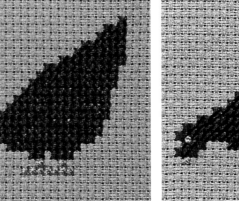

Rhode Island Red Step 1   *Step 2*

BLACK ANCONA

1. Work base in cross-stitch:
   Stitch direction /
   Base – DMC 310 (2), Anchor 401 (1)
   Feet – DMC 729 (2), DMC 783 (1)
   Beak – DMC 725 (3)
2. Rework following the pattern on the graph, using a half cross-stitch:
   Marks – DMC 613 (1)
   Comb – Anchor 13 (3) – cross-stitch
   Eye – DMC 725 (3) – French-knot

◆ It is probably best to work this motif in a good light, as it can sometimes be a bit difficult to see the dark stitches clearly.

RHODE ISLAND RED

1. Work base in cross-stitch:
   Stitch direction \
   Base – DMC 400 (2), DMC 920 (1)
   Feet – DMC 729 (2), DMC 783 (1)
   Beak – DMC 725 (2), DMC 783 (1)
2. Rework following the pattern on the graph, using a half cross-stitch:
   Marks – DMC 3371 (1)
   Comb – Anchor 13 (3) – cross-stitch
   Eye – DMC 725 (3) – French-knot

CORN

Work as French-knots:
Grains – DMC 611 (1), DMC 729 (1), DMC 434 (1)

Welsummer Cockerel

The striking combination of blue/greens and golds have made this colourful cockerel an all-time favourite. The wonderful iridescent quality of the feathers suggests a whole range of colour variations that would be impossible to detail, so I have worked with quite a limited palette to achieve this basic effect. However, you can easily add flecks of brighter colours as highlights, perhaps even a streak of purple, to create a more individual interpretation.

Step 1

Step 2

1. Work the base colours in cross-stitch, changing the direction of the top stitch (Graph 1):
   Stitch direction on body /
   Stitch direction on tail \
   Base colours:
       Body A – DMC 782 (3)
       Body B – DMC 434 (3)
       Body C – DMC 501 (3)
   Tail:
       Green – DMC 500 (3)
       Blue – DMC 796 (3)
   Feet – DMC 782 (2), DMC 729 (1)
   Comb – Anchor 13 (2), DMC 400 (1)
   Beak – DMC 725 (3)

I have included a pattern (*see* page 61 bottom) for the Mill Farm cockerel as he was worked in a similar set of colours and could make an interesting alternative to the Scots Grey in the farm project.

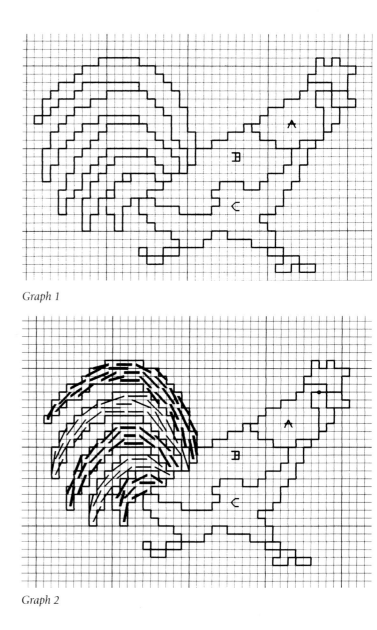

Graph 1

Graph 2

2. Rework the cockerel with a slanting-stitch (*see* page 17) on the body and a long-stitch on the tail. Work the first set of tail colours following the direction of the marks on the graph, and then work the second colour between the stitches, spacing them out so that the base colour just shows through (Graph 2):
   Top-stitch body in slanting-stitch:
       Body A – DMC 676 (1)
       Body B – DMC 783 (1)
       Body C – DMC 320 (1)
   Eye – DMC 310 (3) – French-knot
   Top-stitch tail in long-stitch:
       Green 1 – Anchor 189 (1)
       Green 2 – Anchor 227 (1)
       Blue 1 – Anchor 410 (1)
       Blue 2 – Anchor 189 (1)

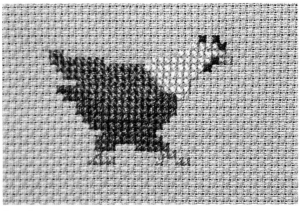

Step 1

Step 2

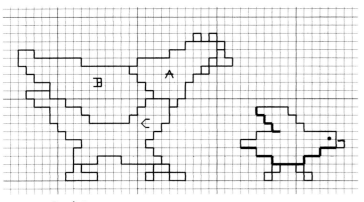

Graph 1

WELSUMMER HEN
1. Work base colours in cross-stitch (Graph 1):
   A and C stitch direction /
   B Stitch direction \
   Base A – DMC 676 (3)
   Base B – DMC 501 (2), DMC 320 (1)
   Base C – DMC 434 (2), DMC782 (1)
   Feet – DMC 729 (2), DMC783 (1)
2. Rework using a half cross-stitch, following pattern on Graph 2:
   Top-stitch A – DMC 434 (1)
   Top-stitch B – DMC 782 (1)
   Top-stitch C – DMC 676 (1)
   Comb – Anchor 13 (3)
   Beak – DMC 725 (3)
   Eye – DMC 310 (3) – French-knot

CHICK
Work in cross-stitch and dark lines on graph in back-stitch:
Body – DMC 676 (1), DMC 612 (1)
Dark lines – DMC 611 (1)
Feet/beak – DMC 729 (3)
Eye – DMC 310 (2) – French-knot

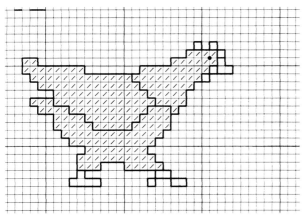

Graph 2

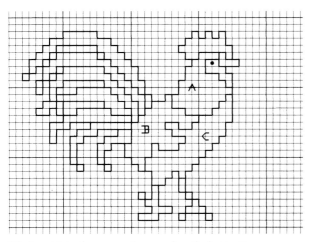

Work graph in the same colours as described opposite.

Detail of cockerel from Mill Farm sampler.

Beehives

The practise of keeping bees in hand-crafted hives was a common activity during the eighteenth and nineteenth centuries, and yet there appears to be surprisingly few examples of the subject being used as an embroidery motif. The few references I have found in some quite early samplers depict a number of miniature bees surrounding a hive that is illustrated in great detail using a variety of stitches, though they all seem to be based on the same style and pattern. A hive worked purely in cross-stitch is even more difficult to find, and it was certainly not a favoured motif in the schoolroom, which may be partly due to the tricky problem of trying to depict the bees successfully. However, during the latter part of the twentieth century, it has become increasingly popular as a subject, but is usually only illustrated in a single colour, which unfortunately has the appearance of seeming rather flat and lacking in character. With this in mind, I have explored various ways of mixing threads and combining stitch techniques to create a number of different designs that do justice to this humble yet fascinating structure.

Coiled Basketwork Beehive

This is probably one of the oldest and simplest forms of beehive, and I have tried to capture the impression of the long grasses that went to make up the coils, by including a shade of dull green into the base colour. To help suggest the different layers of the coils, I have worked the design in alternate shades of the same colour combination, which creates a subtle change of tones that is then reinforced once the coil pattern is applied.

1. Work the base colours in cross-stitch:
   Row A – DMC 434 (2), DMC 370 (1)
   Row B – DMC 370 (2), DMC 434 (1)
   Opening – Anchor 905 (2), DMC 610 (1)
   Table – Anchor 216 (1), DMC 3347 (1),
      DMC 370 (1)
2. Rework across the rows using a diagonal stitch to make the coils. Twist the threads slightly, to hold the colours together:
   Coils – DMC 3046 (1), DMC 676 (1),
      DMC 729 (1)

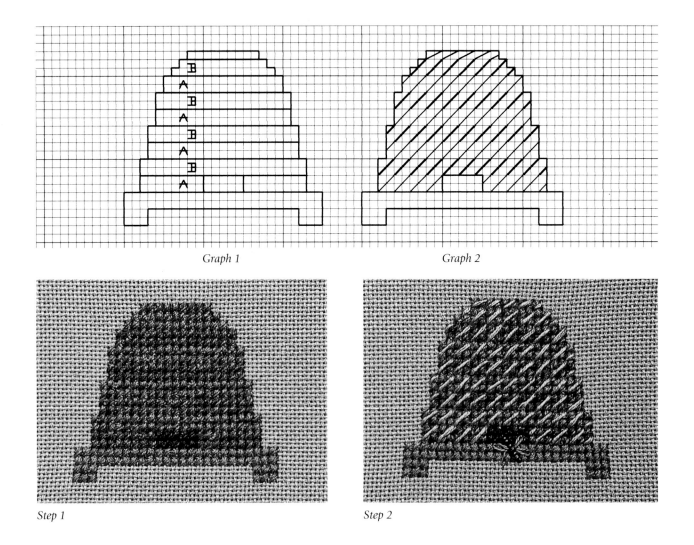

Graph 1   Graph 2

Step 1   Step 2

Wooden Beehive

I found this example of a formal hive in an old gardening book and immediately thought of it as an ideal pattern for embroidering in cross-stitch. The main slats are worked in a mixture of cream and brown colours, which gives a weathered look to the hive and also creates a tactile quality. This is further complemented by using an off-white colour for the narrow dividing bands on the hive and also on the roof.

1. Work in cross-stitch:
    Row A – DMC 613 (1), DMC 612 (1),
       DMC 3047 (1)
    Narrow bands – Anchor 386 (3)
    Roof/legs – Anchor 386 (3)
    Opening – DMC 611 (3)
2. Outline the narrow bands and the lines on the roof in back-stitch:
    Lines – DMC 611 (1)

Straw Beehive

This cottage garden straw skep is worked in a basic cross-stitch. The impression of a texture, and the colour variations of the straw, are achieved by using a combination of shades of thread, and changing the direction of the cross-stitch with the alternating rows.

Row A stitch direction /
Row B stitch direction \

1. Work in cross-stitch:
    Row A – DMC 729 (1), DMC 676 (1),
       DMC 434 (1)
    Row B – DMC 3047 (1), DMC 729 (1),
       DMC 434 (1)
    Opening – DMC 610 (3)
    Table – Anchor 921 (3)
2. Work around opening and between rows A and B with back-stitch, following dark lines on graph:
    Lines – DMC 434 (1), DMC 610 (1) – twist slightly

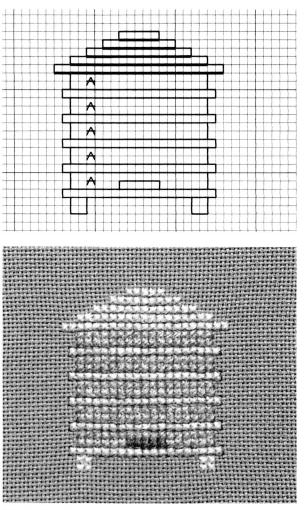

Wooden Beehive

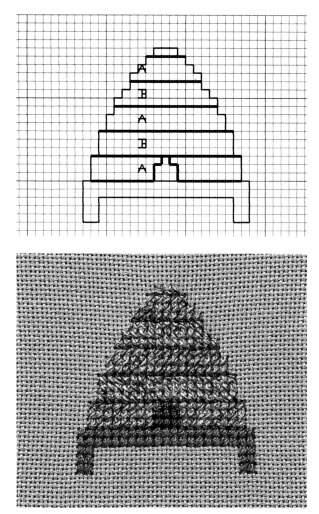

Straw Beehive

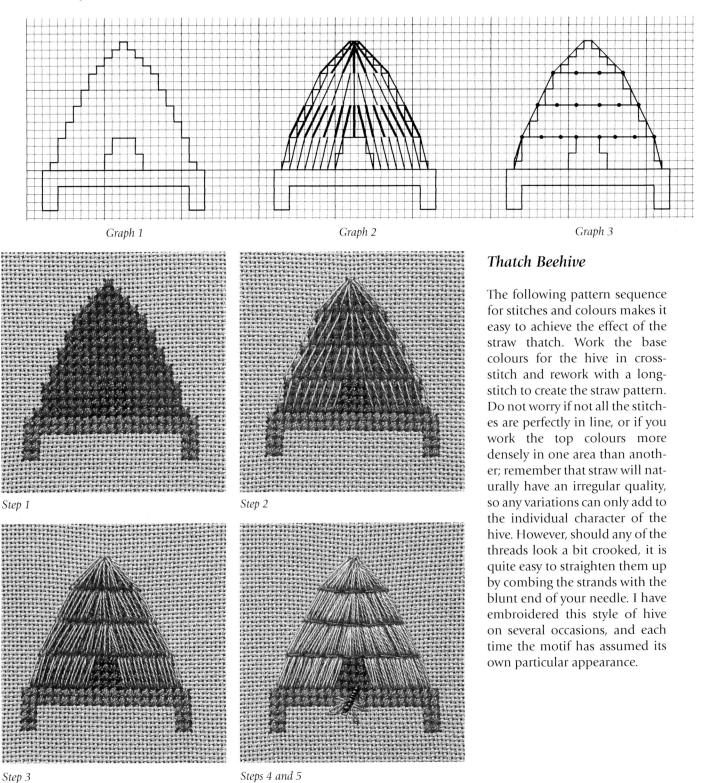

Graph 1   *Graph 2*   *Graph 3*

Step 1   *Step 2*

Step 3   *Steps 4 and 5*

Thatch Beehive

The following pattern sequence for stitches and colours makes it easy to achieve the effect of the straw thatch. Work the base colours for the hive in cross-stitch and rework with a long-stitch to create the straw pattern. Do not worry if not all the stitches are perfectly in line, or if you work the top colours more densely in one area than another; remember that straw will naturally have an irregular quality, so any variations can only add to the individual character of the hive. However, should any of the threads look a bit crooked, it is quite easy to straighten them up by combing the strands with the blunt end of your needle. I have embroidered this style of hive on several occasions, and each time the motif has assumed its own particular appearance.

1. Work the base colours in cross-stitch (Graph 1):
   Hive – DMC 434 (3)
   Door – DMC 610 (3)
   Table – Anchor 921 (3)
2. Work four rows of long-stitch following the direction of the lines in Graph 2:
   First colour – DMC 729 (1)
3. Rework each row, placing the second colour in between the first set of stitches:
   Second colour – DMC 680 (1)

4. Continue working across each row with the third colour, building up the texture:
   Third colour – DMC 676 (1)
5. Finally work lines of back-stitch between the rows, following Graph 3. The dots indicate the length of the stitches:
   Lines – DMC 610 (1), DMC 434 (1)

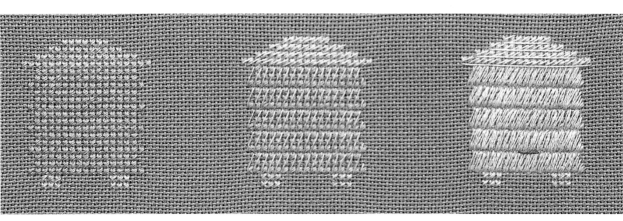

| Step 1 | Step 2 | Step 3 |

Traditional Garden Beehive

The distinctive style of the wooden frame and the reflective qualities of the painted surface are all perfectly illustrated in this example of a typical garden beehive. The use of satin-stitch arranged in rows across the design builds up a smooth and even texture, which transforms the motif; helping to suggest the structure of the form, whilst giving the subject further character and charm.

Graphs 1 and 2   *Graph 3*

1. Work the base colours in cross-stitch following the outline in Graph 1:
   Hive – DMC 613 (2)
   Roof/feet – Anchor 386 (1), DMC 613 (1)
2. Rework the whole motif in a slanted satin-stitch, following the direction of the lines in Graph 2:
   Lines on hive/roof – Anchor 386 (1)

3. Continue with another set of stitches on the hive, placing them between the first set. Work four long lines right across the roof and mark the opening to the hive as in Graph 3:
   Lines across roof – Anchor 386 (1)
   Opening – Anchor 393 (3)

This little scene of small animals, made up a decorative panel in a christening sampler, which featured the family church as the central motif.

The old-fashioned honey pot beehive makes an ideal subject to translate into embroidery. The different styles of the straw and basket-work skeps look so effective and almost real, when their textural quali-ties are re-created through stitches, and the traditional wooden beehive, with its formal and regular structure is also much enhanced, acquiring further character and charm.

5 Meadow Farm

Small motifs of barns and byres with the occasional cow sometimes appear in early English and European samplers, but on the whole the subject of agriculture seems to have been regarded as fairly unimportant. An embroidery devoted entirely to the subject would be rare, and I have only seen one example, where the farm had been recorded in the style of a map with a series of related motifs scattered around the edges. On the other hand, American samplers of the same era display a particular interest in the subject, perhaps arising from their involvement in cultivating and developing a new land. There are many highly imaginative and creative examples, featuring amongst other motifs, herds of cows, farm buildings, fields and even carts and implements.

This project has a farming theme and involves the use of several simple stitch techniques to build up a series of raised surfaces, which help to suggest the actual tactile qualities of the various subjects. The implied flint texture on the barn is actually worked in cross-stitch and looks most effective alongside the soft pinks of the brick-work, giving an added interest to the formal structure of the building. The rich earthy colours used to portray the Friesian cows and sheep echo the colours on the barn and harmonize perfectly with the golden yellows of the corn-stook and wheat borders.

OPPOSITE: This sampler has a slightly more formal appearance, with the solid barn and stretch of meadow grass dominating the lower half of the design. However, a more light-hearted feel could be created, by replacing this area with some small farmyard animals. The two rows including the pigs with geese, and hens with cockerel would fit perfectly into this space, although, the narrow dividing border will need to be changed, to match the colour and style of those already in the design.

Materials Guide

◆ *See* 'Preparing to Work', page 18.
◆ Zweigart fabrics are quoted for all projects.

FABRIC
Aida 14 count Barn Grey
    Fabric size 19 × 21in (49 × 54cm)
    Design size 11½ × 13½in (29 × 34cm)
    Stitch count 155 × 185
Lugana 25 count Pewter
    Fabric size 20 × 22in (50 × 59cm)
    Design size 12 × 14½in (31 × 37cm)
    Stitch count 155 × 185

THREADS
DMC and Anchor (+ denotes full skein):
Green – DMC 580 +, 3012 +, 3013, 3347,
    Anchor 216 +, 855 +, 862 ++
Yellow – DMC 676 ++, 729, 744, 782 ++, 783
Brown – DMC 434, 610, 611, 640 ++, 801, 3371,
    Anchor 310 +, 370, 888 +, 905
White/Beige – DMC 612 +, 613 +, 3823 +,
    Anchor 885 +
Blue – Anchor 920, 939
Pink – DMC 407, Anchor 883
Black/Grey – DMC 310 +, 646, Anchor 401

◆ Mark in guide-lines as described on page 19.
◆ Begin stitching with bottom right-hand corner of the barn and then work in base colour for grass.
◆ The amounts of threads for each colour combination are indicated in brackets (*see* page 20).
◆ The alphabet for this design is no. 5 (*see* page 120).

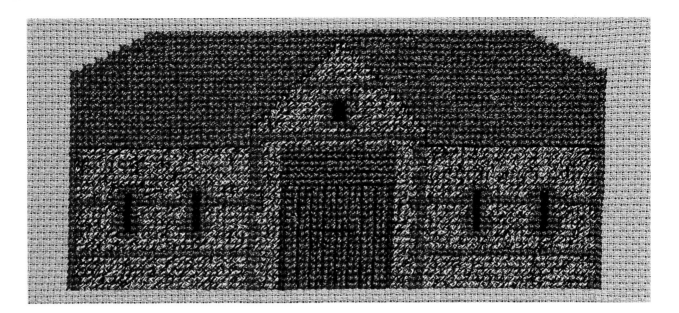

Flint Barn

The monumental stone barns that were once such an intrinsic feature of the farms and villages in the surrounding countryside, have increasingly become an all too rare landmark. With so many having been left to sink into a state of collapse and the ever growing trend for modern conversions, there are few examples that remain in an original condition. Every county has its own particular style of architecture and, combined with the use of local building materials, the buildings from each area acquire an individual character. This example of a flint barn is typical of those found in the south-east, where the local quarries produce a range of stone, varying in tone and colour from mottled browns to hard blacks.

◆ The whole barn is worked almost completely in cross-stitch, with the wonderful varied texture of the black-flint being created by mixing together three contrasting threads and twisting them together as you work. Once you have begun to make the stitches, hold the needle away from the fabric and twist the threads two or three times, then carry on working; this will help to distribute the colours in a more random manner. You will need to repeat this action every so often, in order to keep the twist in the threads. However, you will soon find that you can see a pattern emerging, and if only one of the colours keeps coming up in a particular area, just give the threads an extra twist.

DETAIL ON DOORS

Back-stitch the panels on the doors, following the graph opposite. Work the dark lines in a long back-stitch, over two stitches:
Light lines – DMC 3371 (1)
Dark lines – DMC 310 (1)
Latch – DMC 310 (1), DMC 3371 (1)

BARN

Work the barn in cross-stitch and outline the eaves of the roof in back-stitch (*see* graph opposite):
Black flint – DMC 310 (1), Anchor 888 (1),
    Anchor 885 (1)
Brickwork – DMC 356 (1), DMC 611 (1),
    DMC 434 (1)
Roof – DMC 640 (1), DMC 3012 (1), Anchor 310 (1)
Woodwork – Anchor 905 (1), Anchor 393 (1),
    DMC 646 (1)
Door-posts – Anchor 905 (3)
Window openings – DMC 3371 (2), DMC 310 (1)
Outline eaves of roof – DMC 3371 (1) – back-stitch

GRASS, BEES AND BUTTERFLY

For details *see* pages 83, 95 and 96 respectively.

BORDERS

Narrow band – DMC 676 (1), DMC 782 (1)

LETTERING

Capitals – DMC 434 (1), DMC 611 (1)

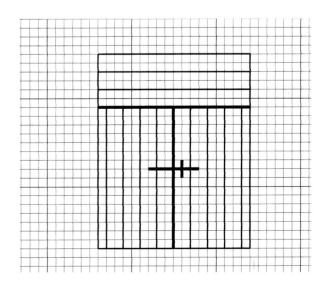

Details for barn door.

Sheep

Spot-motifs depicting the figure of lone sheep appear in some of the earliest recorded English samplers, although their original significance was often largely heraldic in purpose. The inclusion of sheep as part of the composition soon increased in popularity and reflected an interest in pastoral scenes, which had become a common subject in many paintings during the eighteenth and nineteenth centuries.

As samplers gradually became more pictorial, with a classical house as the focal point of the design, large expanses of lawns and fields began to appear across the lower half of the embroidery. These vast areas of green provided an ideal background for displaying groups of animals, and sheep were always a particular favourite. Scenes including a shepherdess attending a flock of sheep not only symbolized a rural idyll, but also probably suggested the status of a family as wealthy landowners. Compositions featuring a house with farm animals, particularly groups of sheep, made an ideal subject for many of the young American girls who were often part of a farming community. Sometimes the sheep were even arranged into neat rows and surrounded by a penned enclosure, which added greatly to the charm and appeal of the particular embroidery, and was in complete contrast to the typical romantic representation of the animal.

The simple and uncomplicated outline of this gentle animal is easily interpreted in cross-stitch, and a line of sheep standing on a narrow band of grass became a favourite pattern of the schoolroom samplers during the nineteenth century. However, many of the earlier examples portray the sheep in a more naturalistic manner, and use the method of outlining the form in back-stitch and then filling in the area with a number of other stitches. Techniques such as chain-stitch, French-knots, and long- and short-stitches all helped to imply a textural surface and give the subject further interest.

Of all the farm animals, sheep must be the most ideally suited to interpretation through embroidery. There are such a variety of breeds, with each one having its own particular textural characteristics, ranging from very tightly packed curls to long straggling locks of wool. I have chosen three different examples to illustrate, and it has been great fun working out how to use some very simple but effective techniques to try and capture the wonderful contrasting qualities of their woollen coats. However, any of the following ideas could be further adapted or experimented with, as once you have worked the basic outline of the sheep in cross-stitch, you do not really need to worry about being too precise with the top-stitches. It is also quite easy to alter the size of the motif, so as to fit in with the overall theme of the design, and the farming scene illustrated below introduces a sense of scale into the composition, with the group of small sheep grazing in a field.

The little sheep, in this detail from a farm commission, were first worked in cross-stitch, using petit point for the faces and feet. I then reworked the bodies with a set of looped stitches, by making a high twist in the thread, before pulling the needle through to the back of the embroidery. This method of working is quite time-consuming and rather fiddly, as you need to repeat the twist action before every stitch, and the threads tend to get knotted very easily. However, the technique makes an interesting and unusual surface texture and is well worth the effort, but is best reserved for small motifs.

Step 1

Step 2

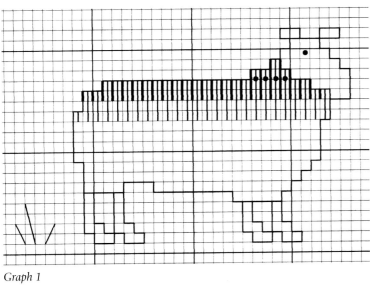

Graph 1

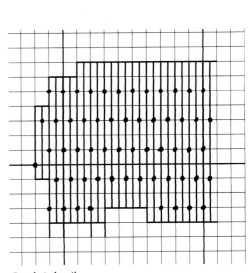

Graph 2 detail

Welsh Black Mountain

There are, in fact, only a few breeds that come under the general heading of black sheep, and of course many of these would actually be in varying shades of blackness. The rich, dark brown colouring of this particular breed brings a wonderful sense of drama to the whole design, and the deep tones are in perfect balance with the other subjects in the composition. The raised surface pattern that is formed from the technique of working rows of straight-stitches in a stepped format, not only suggests a real and implied texture but is also further enhanced by the colour combination of threads.

STRAIGHT-STITCHES ON THE BODY

Following the set of dark lines on Graph 1, work a row of straight-stitches, and then place a second row of stitches between the first. Twist the threads as you work so as to give more structure to the stitch. The detailed Graph 2 shows the pattern of the stitches, which basically form a stepped sequence over four rows of cross-stitch.

◆ Work the base colours in cross-stitch following the outline of the sheep in Graph 1 and then rework the body area using a long straight stitch following the pattern on Graph 2. The dots indicate the length of the stitch.

1. Work in cross-stitch:
   Body – Anchor 905 (2)
   Face and legs – DMC 3371 (3)
2. Rework in long-stitch:
   Body – DMC 610 (1), DMC 801 (1), Anchor 370 (1)
   Eye – DMC 783 (2), DMC 782 (1) – French-knot

TUFTS OF GRASS

The little tufts of grass are worked in a long-stitch using a mixture of three colours. Following the guidelines on Graph 1, place the first set of stitches and then fill in the spaces at random. The flowers are worked as French-knots.

Grass – Anchor 216 (1) and Anchor 855 (1) and
   DMC 3347 (1)
Flowers as for Meadow Grass, *see* page 83.

Suffolk Sheep

The distinctive black face and white curly coat of this particular breed has been so widely illustrated in children's literature that it probably epitomizes most people's idea of a woolly sheep. The use of French-knots as a way of suggesting a surface pattern makes it the obvious choice of technique, particularly as its structure so closely resembles the real texture of the wool. To make more of an impact, I have organized the French-knots into vertical rows spaced between lines of cross-stitch, which helps to create a ridged effect. However, if you prefer, you could quite simply work the sheep motif as a cross-stitch base and then add a series of random French-knots, so as to cover the surface area.

FRENCH-KNOTS ON THE BODY
Working directly onto the fabric, begin the first French-knot one stitch below the top of the design; otherwise the first French-knot will rise above the outline of the sheep's back. Using four strands of thread together, wind the thread round the needle twice, and keeping the stitch quite loose, pull the needle through to the back. As the French-knots are meant to resemble the texture of natural wool, it is not necessary to be too particular about their appearance, which means you can work quite quickly, without worrying about being overly neat and tidy.

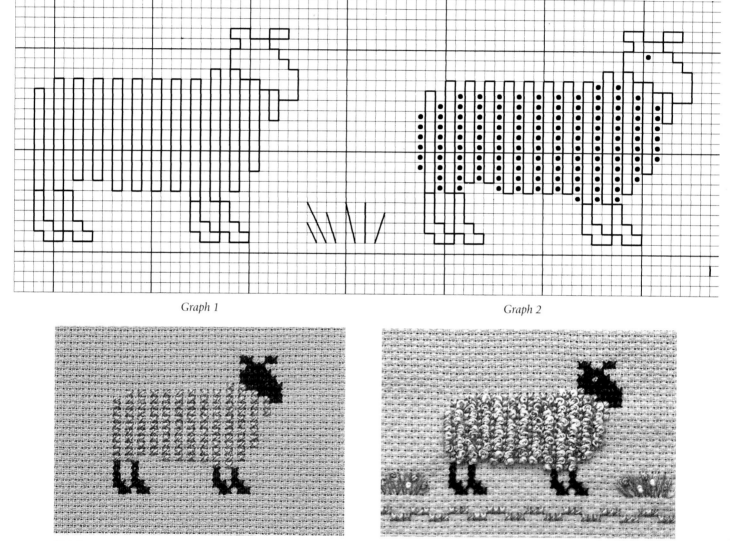

Graph 1   *Graph 2*

Step 1   *Step 2*

◆ Following the pattern on Graph 1 work alternate rows of cross-stitch on the body. Then place a series of French-knots between the vertical lines, using four threads in the needle and working an open knot. *See* the directions above.

1. Work in cross-stitch (Graph 1):
   Body – DMC 613 (2), DMC 640 (1)
   Face and legs – Anchor 905 (2), DMC 3371 (1)
2. Work French-knots (Graph 2):
   Body – DMC 3823 (2), DMC 640 (1), DMC 613 (1)
   Eye – DMC 783 (2), DMC 782 (1)

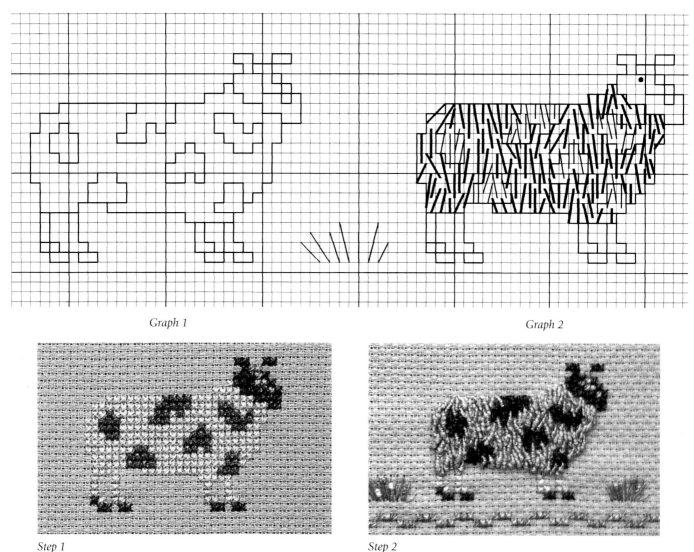

Graph 1   *Graph 2*

Step 1   *Step 2*

◆ Work the base colours in cross-stitch and then rework the body area using a roll-stitch.

1. Work in cross-stitch (Graph 1):
   Body/white – DMC 613 (1), DMC 3823 (1)
   Body/brown – DMC 610 (2)
   Legs – DMC 613 (2), DMC 3823 (1)
   Face/white – DMC 612 (2), DMC 613 (1)
   Face and feet/brown – Anchor 905 (2), DMC 610 (1)

2. Rework in roll-stitch (Graph 2):
   White – DMC 613 (2), DMC 612 (1)
   Brown – Anchor 905 (2), Anchor 610 (1)
   Eye – DMC 783 (2), DMC 782 (1) – French-knot

Jacob Sheep

This breed of sheep is so unusual and striking in its appearance, and made the ideal choice for my third example. The long straggling coat, combined with a varied and random pattern of colouring, provided a wonderful source of reference for translating into embroidery. I decided that the most effective way of illustrating the textural qualities of the wool was to use the technique I call roll-stitch, which would best suggest its naturally unkempt and tangled appearance. Fortunately, for this very reason, you do not have to be too exact about the outcome of each stitch, as any irregularities that occur will add to the overall effect of the textural surface.

ROLL-STITCH ON THE BODY
(*See* the diagram on page 17). Using the pattern on Graph 2 as a guide, place the stitches in a random fashion over the body of the sheep, roughly following the white and brown areas on the cross-stitch base. I have varied the stitch lengths to cover between three and five stitches, with probably the majority being about four stitches in length. The actual roll-stitch can also be varied, so that some of the finished tendrils will appear thicker than others. I have found that by working round the straight-stitches, between five and ten times, creates enough variation.

Milk Churn and Skylark

A delightful scene depicting a milk-maid, carrying a yoke with pails and standing next to a cow, appears in a number of early Dutch and German samplers. The patterns are usually worked in cross-stitch and there seems to be several variations on the theme, including a farmer and his wife with milk churns and pails, together with a large cow. Occasionally, similar motifs occur in English embroideries, which does suggest that patterns were available to teachers and pupils alike, but perhaps the subject was just not considered as fashionable and appealing, particularly compared to the formal house and garden compositions. Many American samplers of the same period demonstrate a keen interest in the whole area, displaying a sympathetic interpretation of the subject, with great attention to detail. The motifs were usually outlined in back-stitch and filled in with other stitches, so as to create a more realistic style of motif. One piece of work might feature several cows grazing in a field and various farm workers, including a milk-maid, carrying a pail balanced on her head, and also a seated figure milking a cow, beside a bucket. An array of patterns and colours were used to distinguish the various breeds of dairy cows, and scenes including a pair of large oxen pulling a hay-cart were also very popular.

Milk Churn

This pretty milk churn, in the typical blue and cream dairy colours, makes a decorative addition to the design.

◆ Work the base colours in cross-stitch and then rework in satin-stitch, following the pattern on Graph 2. Then place a second set of stitches between the first set.

Churn/blue – Anchor 920 (2) – cross-stitch
  First set of satin-stitch – Anchor 920 (1)
  Second set of satin-stitch – Anchor 939 (1)
Churn/white – DMC 3823 (2) – cross-stitch
  – both sets of satin-stitch – DMC 3823 (1)
Paddle – DMC 640 (1) – outline in long-stitch and
  fill in with small straight stitches

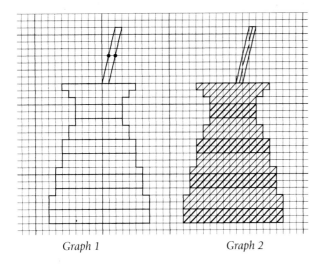

| *Graph 1* | *Graph 2* |

| *Step 1* | *Step 2* |

Skylark

The familiar sight of a skylark hovering above the fields and pastures, makes this little bird the perfect choice for including in a farm scene.

1. Base – cross-stitch (Graph 1):
   A Wings and tail – DMC 612 (1), DMC 611 (1)
   B Body – DMC 612 (2)
   White on tail – DMC 613 (1), DMC 3823 (1)
2. Rework details (Graph 2):
   A marks – DMC 434 (1), Anchor 905 (1)
   B marks – DMC 434 (1)
   Beak and crown – Anchor 905 (1) –
     straight-stitch
   Eye – DMC 3371 (2) – French-knot

◆ Work base colours in cross-stitch and rework details, following the marks on the graph, using small straight-stitches

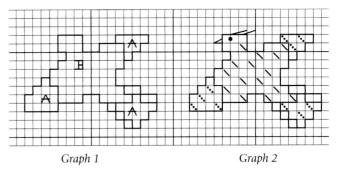

| *Graph 1* | *Graph 2* |

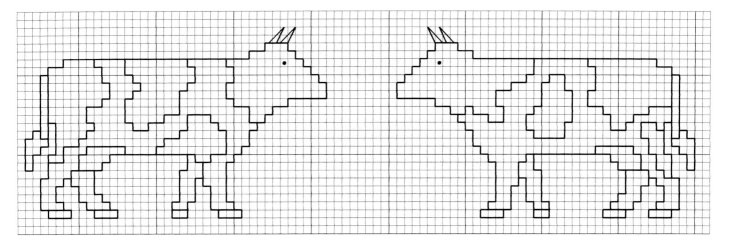

Cows

The characteristic bold markings that distinguish the Friesian and Ayrshire breeds make them ideal subjects for adding interest to a composition, and I usually try to match the particular colouring of each animal with the overall colour scheme of the design. The strong black and white patterns on the Friesian cow perfectly complement the colours of the black flint in the barn, although I have actually had to combine several different threads in order to create a more harmonious expression of these two contrasting shades. Placing two such intense colours next to each other, and simply using basic black and white threads, could make them appear rather startling and unrealistic, whereas by introducing a brown and grey into the black, and light browns into the white areas, a more muted and subtle effect is achieved.

Both the cows are worked in cross-stitch, and an impression of texture is created by changing the angle of the top stitch on each motif, so that the light catches the different direction of the stitches. The horns are outlined in back-stitch, and the area filled in with a series of small straight-stitches, adding a delicate detail to the design.

FRIESIAN COWS
Work the following colours in cross-stitch, slanting the top stitch in opposite directions:
Left cow / stitch direction
Right cow \ stitch direction
Black – DMC 310 (1), Anchor 905 (1),
 Anchor 401 (1)
White – DMC 3823 (1), DMC 613 (1), DMC 612 (1)
Hooves – DMC 610 (2), DMC 612 (1)
Udders – DMC 407 (2), DMC 612 (1)
Legs/shadow – DMC 612 (2), DMC 613 (1)
Eye – Anchor 370 (2), DMC 610 (2) – French-knot,
 twice round needle
Horns – Anchor 905 (1) – outline in back-stitch and
 fill in with long-/short-stitch – DMC 610 (1)

The rich brown tones of the Ayrshire breed make an alternative option for the project, and could be used to replace the black areas in the patterns.

LEFT: *In this example of an Ayrshire cow, I have used a different technique for portraying the smooth surface of the animal's coat. By over-stitching the cross-stitch base with a slanting-stitch, the impression of a sleek texture is created, which also disguises the square structure of the cross-stitch. As the actual colour of the breeds is so variable, the choice of which particular brown and white shades you choose can be adjusted according to the basic colour theme in your design. In this instance I used quite a reddish brown, so as to suggest a rich chestnut colouring, and a shade such as Anchor 355 for the cross-stitch base could be reworked with something like DMC 400 for the slanting-stitch. Similarly the white areas could be worked in a combination of Ecru coloured tones.*

Corn Stooks

The evocative image of a solitary corn stook has symbolized the farming countryside for generations, and in spite of our industrialized society, many families still feel that their roots are in the land. It is therefore not surprising that there remains such a strong connection and association with the romantic idyll of rural life. The picturesque qualities of the corn stook have an immediate appeal, and translate most effectively when interpreted in embroidery; although it features extremely rarely in the history of sampler making. I have seen a few beautifully executed examples in both English and American embroideries, but obviously a subject as intricate and detailed as this would have seemed quite daunting to all but the most confident of needle-workers. I doubt very much that there were any patterns, beyond printed illustrations to work from, so it would have been up to each individual to interpret the subject in their own style. Certainly it is too complex a structure to have much meaning in cross-stitch alone, and needs the addition of a few other simple stitches to bring it to life.

My first attempts at a corn stook were in the Burton Common sampler, where I wanted to include a group of stooks to suggest the fields behind my cottage. I designed a small and very simple motif that was very easy to improvise upon, once the basic cross-stitch outline was in place. I then decided I wanted something more elaborate in the Mill Farm sampler, and initially worked from some sketches directly onto the embroidery fabric. This example was very stylized and formal in appearance, and I have made a variation on this design for the corn stook that features in the Meadow Farm project.

The little stooks featured below look most effective when placed together as a group, and the slight variations in each motif give them a more natural appearance. In fact any differences between the colours and stitches, particularly the French-knots, create a more exciting individual interpretation. I have planned a sequence of graph patterns that describe the basic stages of the stitches, and it is quite easy to alter the scale of the motif to suit the requirements of your design.

A detail showing the group of small stooks in the field, from the Burton Common sampler.

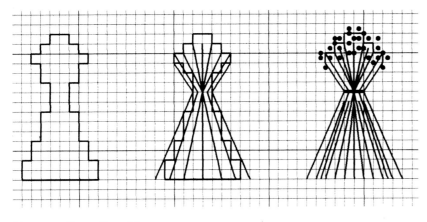

Basic graph pattern for the small stooks featured above. Follow the directions for colours and stitches below and on page 77.

Burton Corn Stook

1. Work the base colour in cross-stitch – DMC 434 (2)
2. Following the lines on Graph 2, work the first set of long-stitches – DMC 676 (1)
3. Make another set of long-stitches, working between the first set – DMC 680 (1) (Graph 3)
4. Continue to build up the surface with another set of stitches – DMC 729 (1) (Step 4)

◆ Rework with DMC 676 (1), filling in any obvious gaps. At this stage the stitches can be spaced quite randomly.

◆ Band – DMC 676 (1), DMC 434 (1) – work five horizontal long-stitches across the centre to form the band – to get the best colour effect, do not let the threads twist together (Graph 4).

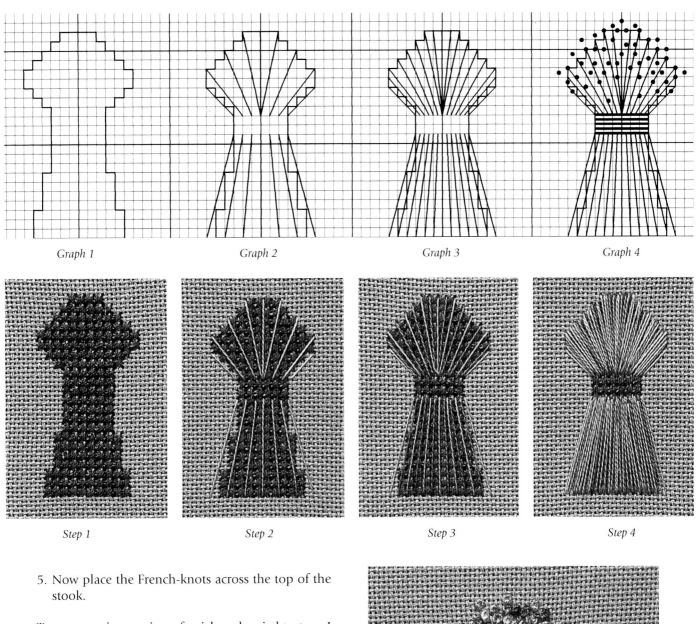

Graph 1   Graph 2   Graph 3   Graph 4

Step 1   Step 2   Step 3   Step 4

5. Now place the French-knots across the top of the
   stook.

To create an impression of a rich and varied texture, I
have used four threads in each French-knot, and also
five different colour combinations. Begin with the first
group of colours and place a number of French-knots
around the area, and then work between them with
the second colour, and so on. I have charted some
positions on Graph 4 as a guide, but you need not follow them exactly, as each stook will end up having its
own individual character.

The five groups of colours for the French-knots – use
four threads together in the needle:
– DMC 434 (2), DMC 680 (2)
– DMC 676 (3), DMC 729 (1)
– DMC 676 (2), DMC 729 (1), DMC 680 (1)
– DMC 676 (2), DMC 680 (1), DMC 434 (1)
– DMC 744 (3), DMC 676 (1)

Step 5

Meadow Farm Corn Stook

In this very decorative and stylized design, I have made a feature of the characteristic upright stance of the stook by arranging the stalks into a series of parallel lines to form a geometric pattern. The alternating colours of the cross-stitch base are totally transformed by the addition of the narrow lines of long-stitch, and the high twist on the threads makes a distinctive twill pattern that creates a rich surface of colour and texture. The ears of corn are suggested by the soft natural forms of the lazy-daisy stitch, which contrast perfectly with the formal style of the base.

CORN STOOK
1. Cross-stitch the base in vertical lines of alternate colours:
   Dark – DMC 434 (2), DMC 729 (1)
   Light – DMC 782 (1), DMC 729 (1), DMC 676 (1)

Work long back-stitch lines for the positions of the corn; the dots on Graph 1 represent the length of each stitch – DMC 434 (1)

2. Following the pattern on Graph 2, use a lazy-daisy stitch to form the ears of corn – I find it easiest to work up one side of the stalk and then back down the other side:
   Dark corn – DMC 434 (1), DMC 729 (1)

◆ Overstitch the cross-stitch base with a long-stitch, that travels the full length of the dark lines indicated on the graph – work top and bottom halves separately.

◆ Twist the thread about six to seven times to create a twill texture – you will probably need to re-twist the thread, when you are one-third and two-thirds through the procedure – DMC 676 (2).

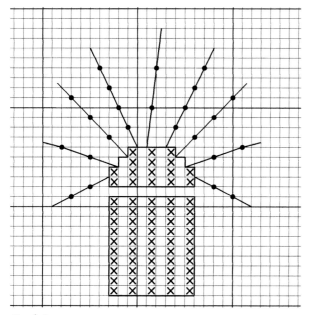

Graph 1

Graph 2

Step 1

Step 2

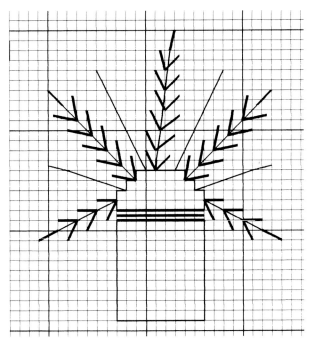

Graph 3

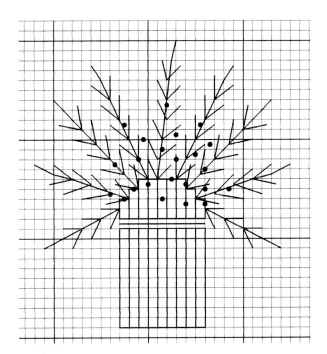

Graph 4

Step 3

Step 4

 Use the graph patterns 2 and 3 as a guide for positioning the ears of corn, but do not worry if some of the stitches are not placed in exactly the same positions or vary slightly in size. The short lines, which represent each ear of corn, indicate the actual length of the needle points in the fabric, with the little stitch at the end of the lazy-daisy being added on afterwards. All the patterns for the stooks are quite easy to adapt or interpret in your own way, and you can see that the corn stook in the Mill Farm sampler is an elaborated combination of these two styles.

3. Work the lighter set of corn in the same way, continuing with lazy-daisy stitch (Graph 3):
Light corn – DMC 676 (1), DMC 782 (1)

 Using four threads together, work three long-stitches horizontally across the stook to form the band – twist the thread in the needle four times, to create a colour change in the stitch:
Band – DMC 744 (2), DMC 434 (1), DMC 676 (1)

4. Now work a series of French-knots, roughly following the positions on the graph – twist the thread twice to make a closed knot, and wind once round the needle:
French-knots – DMC 744 (2), DMC 676 (1)

79

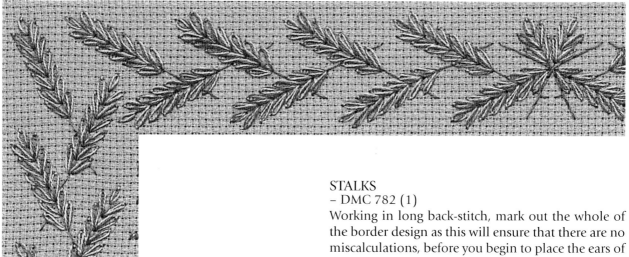

STALKS
– DMC 782 (1)

Working in long back-stitch, mark out the whole of the border design as this will ensure that there are no miscalculations, before you begin to place the ears of corn. The length of each stitch is indicated by the dots on the graph pattern below.

EARS OF CORN
– DMC 782 (1), DMC 676 (1)

◆ Cut the two threads to a length of about 21in (54cm), as this is just enough to complete one set of lazy-daisy stitches on the ear of corn.

◆ Make a row of lazy-daisy stitches up one side of the stalk, towards the top, and then work back downwards.

◆ The length of each lazy-daisy stitch on the graph below indicates the points of the needle in the fabric, the little stitch at the top is added on afterwards.

◆ In order to keep the ears of corn an equal length, one set of lazy-daisy needs to be worked over 3½ stitches (note the horizontal lines in graph pattern).

◆ Keep the threads untwisted, as this allows the light to catch the threads and create a naturally changing pattern of colour.

Corn Border

The pattern for this striking border design is so simple and easy to work, involving the use of only two basic stitches. The positions of the stalks are firstly marked out in long back-stitch, and then the ears of corn are added, using a lazy-daisy stitch. Most borders can be quite time consuming, and although this appears quite an intricate pattern, it actually takes no longer than a cross-stitch design, of a similar scale.

This border is quite easy to extend, should you wish to include more text. Alternatively, you could just work the top and bottom sections of the border and leave out the side-panels, if you felt there was too much work or had a limited area for a particular design. This would still capture the atmosphere of the corn motif, and a narrow cross-stitch band worked in similar colours could be placed up the sides of the embroidery.

Details for the centre section of the top border. The dots on the graph indicate the length of the stitches.

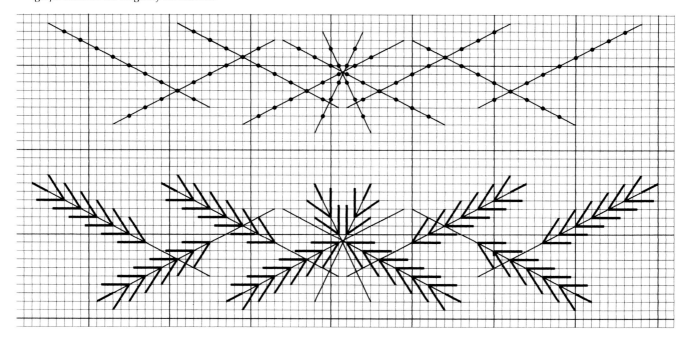

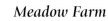

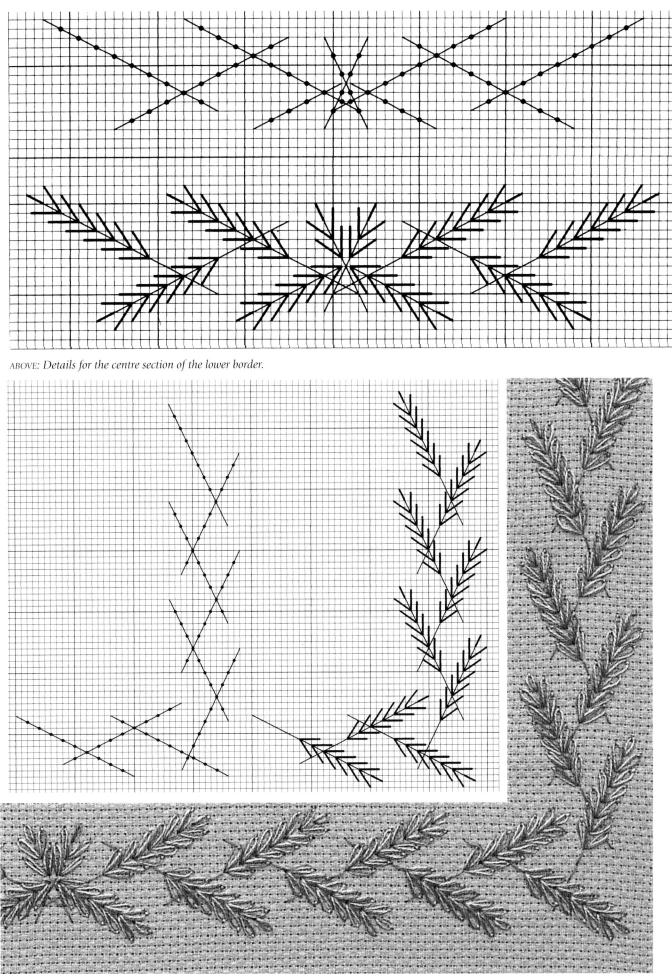

ABOVE: *Details for the centre section of the lower border.*

Details for the lower corner sections and side panels.

Grasses

Vast stitched areas of vibrant greens, filled with animals and figures, sometimes covering almost a third of the whole design, are one of the most striking and dominant features of many eighteenth-century samplers. Although this form of composition was particularly favoured in American embroideries, it was also quite widely practised in English samplers, only on a more conservative scale. The popular subject of a house, fronted with an area of lawn, may well have originated in England, but it was the flamboyant style of the American schools that took the idea a step further. Rather than working these large areas in cross-stitch alone, a number of other techniques were combined with a wide range of colours to create an exciting surface of real and implied texture.

This detail from the Meadow Farm project, shows the grass worked as an area of cross-stitch in the base colours, before being re-worked in long-stitch.

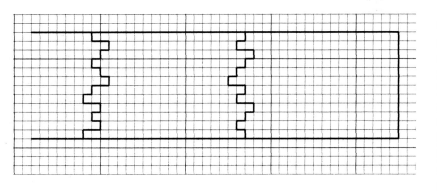

Staggering rows of stitching helps to blend the colours.

The dark green base for the grass is best worked in small sections of about nineteen stitches wide, so as to avoid creating a tension on the fabric. Very long rows of cross-stitch can cause the threads to tighten up and for the embroidery to pull in at the sides. The graph, left, shows the edges of the short rows arranged in a staggered pattern to make the joins less obvious. This technique for stepping the edges of your rows can be applied to any design that covers a large area, such as roofs of buildings and expanses of water.

Alternative Colour Scheme for the Grass Worked as Cross-Stitch

This example shows the grass worked in cross-stitch, using a combination of three tones of green to imply a varied texture, and could make an easier alternative to the technique described on the page opposite. I have also used slightly brighter colours for the flowers, to make them stand out from the grass, and once they are in place, you could always work a few straight-stitches along the front of the grass to add some extra texture.

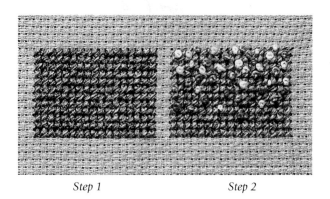

Step 1   *Step 2*

STEP 1
GRASS
Work in cross-stitch:
– DMC 734 (1), DMC 3051 (1), Anchor 216 (1)

STEP 2
FLOWERS
Work as French-knots:
Yellow – DMC 783 (1), DMC 782 (1), DMC 676 (1)
Blue – Anchor 939 (2), DMC 825 (1)
White – DMC 3823 (2), DMC 746 (1)

Meadow Grass

This technique for building up an area of grass is so easy to follow and gives a wonderful tactile quality to the work. The use of the long- and short-stitches closely resembles the upright direction of the grass, and the layers of different colours add interest and create real depth to what would otherwise be a uniform tone of green.

I have included quite a large area of grass at the base of the barn, as I wanted to suggest the atmosphere of a meadow, carpeted with delicate wild flowers. Although this design might appear to involve quite a lot of work, do not be put off too soon, as it is not as laborious as it first seems, and the final results are well worth the effort. Once you have completed the cross-stitch base and the first set of long stitches, the following stages are much quicker, as the additional colours are spaced further apart. However, if you feel you would prefer something less intricate, you could still achieve a similar effect with just cross-stitch, by using a combination of colours to create a flecked texture (*see* details opposite).

FLOWERS
The little flowers are worked as French-knots, using three colours, and can be added in a random fashion. Starting at the right-hand side of the grass, work across the area, placing the knots closer together at the top of the grass and spacing them out more as you work down. This will create the illusion of depth and give the feeling of the grass coming towards you. I found it easiest to load up three needles with the colours and work them across together, placing the blue flowers slightly further apart than the white and yellow, and keeping them more to the foreground. It is probably best to put too few rather than too many initially, as you can always come back and add more to fill in any gaps. The dots in the right-hand graph below give a rough guide to the spacing of the flowers.

Work as French-knots:
Yellow – DMC 676 (1), DMC 744 (1), DMC 782 (1)
Blue – Anchor 939 (2), Anchor 920 (1)
White – DMC 3823 (3)

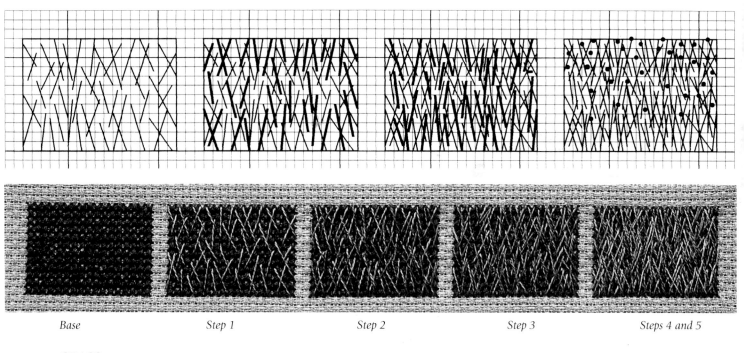

| Base | Step 1 | Step 2 | Step 3 | Steps 4 and 5 |

GRASS
First work the base colour in cross-stitch, and then build up the five sets of colours using a long-stitch. The marks in the graph pattern give you a guide as to where to place the stitches, but any variations in colour and texture will only add to the individual character of the embroidery.

Base – Anchor 862 (2) – cross-stitch
1– Anchor 855 (1) – long-stitch
2– DMC 580 (1)
3– Anchor 216 (1)
4– DMC 3013 (1)
5– DMC 3347 (1)

Detail of the expanse of meadow grass from the Meadow Farm project.

Stylized Grass

Here is a very quick and effective way of making an exciting textural surface that implies the structural qualities of grass, but in a decorative form. The method of placing rows of straight-stitches together to form a stylized pattern was the most popular technique in use during the eighteenth and nineteenth centuries, and was sometimes worked over almost a third of the design. This simple technique is so versatile and flexible, with endless possibilities to combine any amount of colours with a number of different patterns. For instance, the embroidery example below explains the basic technique, but the choice of colours and sequence of stitches are only two of many variables. As there are really no set rules, you can have great fun experimenting, and here are a few ideas you may want to consider.

The tonal strength of the base colour could be varied considerably. I have suggested a base that is quite similar to the top colours, but a much darker shade, or even a brown coloured base, would make quite a difference to the overall appearance of the motif.

The length of the stitches can add another dimension to the subject. Whether each row is the same width, or perhaps they alternate between wide and narrow lines, similarly the rows could be graduated from a narrow width at the top and then becoming wider as you get to the bottom. Also a more expressive and individual interpretation could be achieved by adding small amounts of other colours in a random fashion, once the basic set of stitches have been worked.

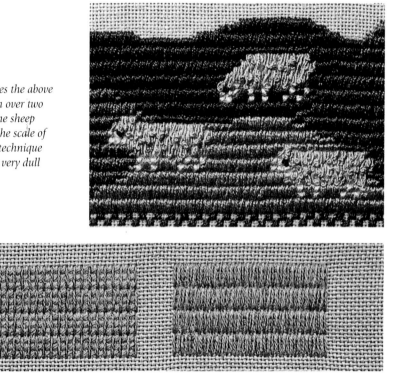

RIGHT: A group of sheep grazing in the fields illustrates the above technique perfectly. I have used a straight satin-stitch over two rows of cross-stitch and worked the pattern around the sheep motifs. The smaller width of stitch is more suited to the scale of the subject and the three-dimensional quality of the technique brings interest and life to what would otherwise be a very dull and monotonous area.

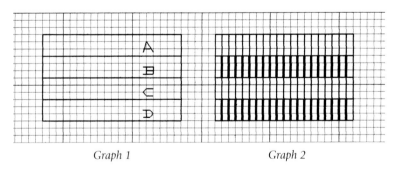

Step 1 *Step 2* *Step 3*

Graph 1 *Graph 2*

GRASS COLOURS
1. Base A and C – DMC 3347 (2)
   Base B and D – DMC 502 (2)
2. Rework with first colour:
   A and C – DMC 502 (2)
   B and D – DMC 320 (2)
3. Rework with second colour:
   A and C – DMC 320 (1), DMC 503 (1)
   B and D – DMC 3347 (2)

◆ Work the base colours in cross-stitch. Rework each row with two sets of colours, using a satin-stitch and placing the second colour between the first set of stitches. Follow the pattern of the lines on Graph 2 for the first set of stitches.

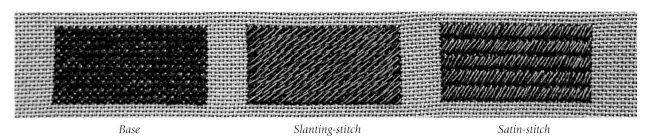

| Base | Slanting-stitch | Satin-stitch |

Textured Grass

This is another easy technique that transforms a piece of plain cross-stitch, and gives added character to a design. I find that a small area of textured grass, placed at the base of a house or church, always helps to complement the warm earthy colours and formal structure of the building. As with the technique discussed on the opposite page, any number of alternative approaches could be explored and a more decorative effect could be achieved with the addition of some small flowers, similar to those worked in the Meadow Farm project. However, if you wanted to include other subjects, such as little animals or birds within the grass area, then you need to work the patterns into the design at the cross-stitch stage. Once the motifs are in place you can then build up the various textures separately, although you will probably find it easier to work in the grass textures first.

This detail from a family portrait, shows just how an area of grass can be used as a way of linking the central motif of the house with the figures and tree in the garden.

GRASS
1. Base – Anchor 879 (2) – cross-stitch
2. Top-stitch – Anchor 216 (1) – slanting-stitch
3. Top-stitch – Anchor 216 (1) – satin-stitch
   Second colour – DMC 320 (1)

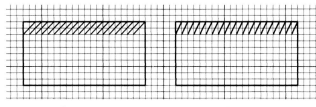

| Graph for slanting-stitch | Graph for satin-stitch |

◆ I have illustrated two slightly different approaches here, although both are worked on the same dark-coloured base. The first example is worked in slanting-stitch, and shows the technique I used for the grass in the Country House project. The second example is a variation on the technique described on the opposite page, with the rows of satin-stitches being angled in a slanting direction.

6 Woodland Animals

Many examples of English spot samplers are scattered with a variety of motifs depicting indigenous wild animals. The squirrel and deer were the most popular subjects, and were either included for the symbolic meanings that were attached to them, or alternatively used simply as a way of filling in an odd space. The scale of the motifs in comparison to the other elements in the design was seemingly unimportant, and they were usually portrayed in an assortment of stylized and formal poses.

Woodland animals have always been surrounded with myth and legend; their secret nocturnal lives creating a sense of mystery and wonder. To try and capture some of these feelings in the design, and suggest an atmosphere of evening twilight, I have placed several small moths hovering amongst the animals; their amazing colour schemes adding a magical quality to the whole composition.

Rows of cross-stitch alphabets and numerals were a common feature of many schoolroom samplers, and always bring a particular charm to an embroidery. With this in mind, I decided to arrange the numbers from one to ten, in the way of letter-forms, around the edge of the design. To create a sense of movement, I alternated the three shades of blue, and made a pattern with the light and dark colours as they travel round the border.

OPPOSITE: The usual decorative and floral themes of the sampler embroidery can sometimes make it difficult to find a design that would be suitable for a little boy. However, the colours and motifs of this woodland composition would make an ideal choice, and also create much interest and appeal once he was older. Alternatively, the farmyard design could be adapted slightly by altering the colour schemes of the alphabet and borders.

Materials Guide

- *See* 'Preparing to Work', page 18.
- Zweigart fabrics are quoted for all projects.

FABRIC
Lugana 25 count Fawn
    Fabric size 19½ × 23in (49.5 × 59cm)
    Design size 11½ × 15in (29 × 38cm)
    Stitch count 145 × 193
Aida 14 count Barn Grey
    Fabric size 18¾ × 22in (47.5 × 56.5cm)
    Design size 10½ × 14in (27 × 36cm)
    Stitch count 145 × 193

THREADS
DMC and Anchor (+ denotes full skein):
Green – DMC 500, 501, 370, 3347, Anchor 216 +
Yellow – DMC 676, 725, 729, 783, 3046
Grey – DMC 646
Brown – DMC 434 +, 435 +, 610 +, 611 +, 612 +, 801, 3045, 3371 +, Anchor 369, 373 +, 392, 393, 831 +, 905
Red/pink – DMC 316 +, 355, 407 +, 632, Anchor 13, 884 +
Blue – Anchor 920 ++, 921 ++, 922 +
White – DMC 3823, 613

- Mark in guide-lines as described on page 19.
- Count up and place in narrow border below house. Begin with tree or house.
- The amounts of threads in each colour combination are indicated in brackets (*see page 20*).
- The alphabet for this design is no. 4 (*see* page 120).

House and Deer

The woodland setting for this little house, as it nestles amongst the fir-trees, helps to suggest a narrative theme to the embroidery and makes a descriptive focal point for the whole composition. There is a sense of the day ending and evening approaching as the pheasants fly off to roost and the various nocturnal animals emerge from their dens. In the pine branches the squirrels are retiring as the owls make their appearance, and the dancing hares have come out to play, whilst the three larger animals make a bold statement at the bottom of the design. The soft muted pink colouring of the building gives it a picturesque and almost toy-like appearance, and adds to the fantasy element of the composition. However, if you prefer a more realistic-looking building, you could quite easily substitute a brick pattern, following the colour combinations that are described in the other projects that include details for building materials.

FALLOW DEER
Work in cross-stitch following graph on opposite page:
Body – DMC 434 (1), DMC 610 (1), Anchor 369 (1)
Spots – Anchor 831 (2), DMC 3823 (1)
Antlers – Anchor 905 (1), Anchor 392 (1), DMC 611 (1)
Eye – DMC 3371 (3)

TREES
Work in cross-stitch:
Trunk/dark green branches – Anchor 216 (3)
Light green branches – DMC 3347 (3)

BEEHIVES AND BEES
See pages 62 and 95.

MOTHS
See page 98.

Graph patterns for house and tree are shown opposite.

HOUSE
Work in cross-stitch:
Walls – DMC 407 (1), DMC 316 (1), DMC 612 (1)
Roof – DMC 632 (2), DMC 355 (1)
Window panes – DMC 646 (2)
Door – Anchor 392 (2), DMC 3045 (1)
Window frame and door frame – DMC 3823 (2), Anchor 831 (1)
Window bars – DMC 3823 (2) – long-stitch
Door knob – DMC 646 (3) – French-knot

BORDERS
Work in cross-stitch:
Narrow blue – Anchor 921 (2), Anchor 920 (1)
White spots – DMC 3823 (3)

ALPHABET
Work in cross-stitch:
Dark blue – Anchor 922 (2)
Medium blue – Anchor 921 (2)
Light blue – Anchor 920 (2)

LETTERING
Work in cross-stitch:
Text – DMC 612 (1), DMC 611 (1)

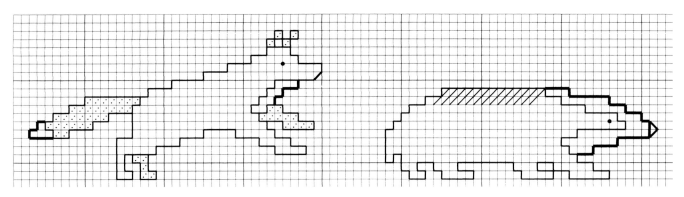

Fox and Badger

Various motifs depicting a fox running or skulking around, appear in a number of compositions, but there seem to be no references to the badger in early samplers, and even today it is not a very common embroidery motif. The use of slanting-stitch provides an ideal way of making a real surface texture in one colour, whilst allowing the darker base colour to show through, and suggests the distinctive quality of the animal's coat. However, if you would rather work in just cross-stitch, quite a nice effect can still be achieved by combining some darker and lighter shades, to make a varied textural pattern on the body.

Cross-stitch colours – DMC 3371 (1), DMC 310 (1), Anchor 392 (1)

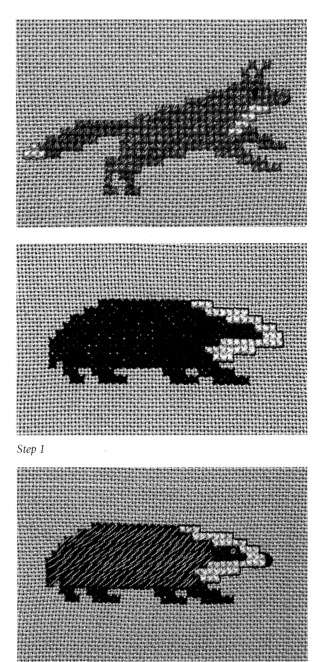

Step 1

Step 2

FOX

Work in cross-stitch, and outline white areas in back-stitch:

Fox body – Anchor 884 (1), Anchor 373 (1),
   DMC 435 (1)
Tail and ears, and feet in shadow – DMC 435 (1),
   DMC 611 (1), Anchor 884 (1)
White on throat and tip of tail – DMC 3823 (2),
   Anchor 831 (1)
Outline white areas – DMC 435 (1) – back-stitch
Eye – DMC 3371 (3) – French-knot
Nose – DMC 3371 (3) – half a cross-stitch

BADGER

Work in cross-stitch:

1. Dark brown body – DMC 3371 (2), Anchor 905 (1)
   White head – DMC 3823 (2), Anchor 831 (1)
   Outline white – Anchor 905 (1) – back-stitch
2. Rework body – Anchor 393 (1) – slanting-stitch
   (*see* page 17)
   Eye – DMC 783 (3) – French-knot
   Nose – DMC 3371 (2) – back-stitch and fill in
   with small stitches.

◆ The graph pattern above shows the first line of diagonal stitches. Move down one cross-stitch row to begin the next line of stitches. It is easiest to work from the head end towards the tail, using a new length of thread for each line of stitches.

Pheasants

The subject of birds in general has been used as a source of inspiration for embroiderers throughout the history of sampler making. Realistic representations of particular species have been equally as popular as more stylized imaginary versions, and the scale and intricacy of the motifs has varied considerably: ranging from very small simple cross-stitch forms, to larger highly detailed examples worked in a variety of techniques. The wonderful array of patterns and markings that is the characteristic feature of each individual bird, can pose a number of problems when trying to include all the information into a small space. I have tried to combine the two different approaches previously mentioned, by working the basic outline of the bird in cross-stitch, and then overstitching the area with a series of smaller stitches, so as to illustrate all the details of the colours and patterns.

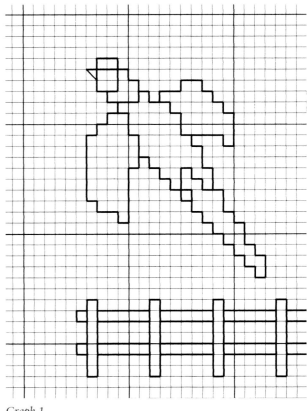

Graph 1

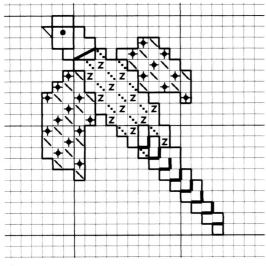

Graph 2

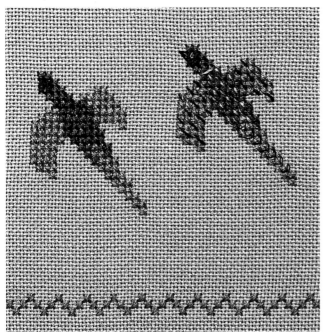

PHEASANTS
Work base colours in cross-stitch, and angle the top stitch to the left (Graph 1):
Bird's stitch direction \

1. Brown on body – DMC 434 (2), DMC 610 (1)
   Wings and tail – Anchor 373 (2), DMC 435 (1)
   Green on head – DMC 501 (3)
   Red on head – DMC 355 (3)
2. Rework body and wings using a half cross-stitch – follow colour symbols on Graph 2:

Body:
▪▪ – Anchor 831 (2)
✦ – DMC 355 (1), DMC 783 (1)
Wings:
Z – DMC 355 (1), DMC 3371 (1)
\ – DMC 783 (1), DMC 434 (1)
Rework tail using a back-stitch
   Dark lines – Anchor 831 (1), DMC 3371 (1)
   Eye – DMC 783 (2) – French-knot
   Beak – DMC 3371 (1) – back-stitch – outline and
      fill in with one stitch.
White collar on throat – Anchor 831 (2) – straight-
   stitch.

FENCE
Work in cross-stitch:
White fence – DMC 3823 (2)

This detail shows the pheasant in its base colours on the left, and the finished motif on the right.

Owls and Squirrels

First work the owls in cross-stitch, remembering to change the direction of the top stitch. Then rework the details, following the patterns on the graph. A single French-knot makes a nice beady eye, and twist the threads to make a more defined beak.

The squirrels are worked in cross-stitch, and the random pattern of the colours combined with the different direction of the stitches makes a lively and varied textural surface. Follow the graph on the opposite page, outlining the white areas in back-stitch.

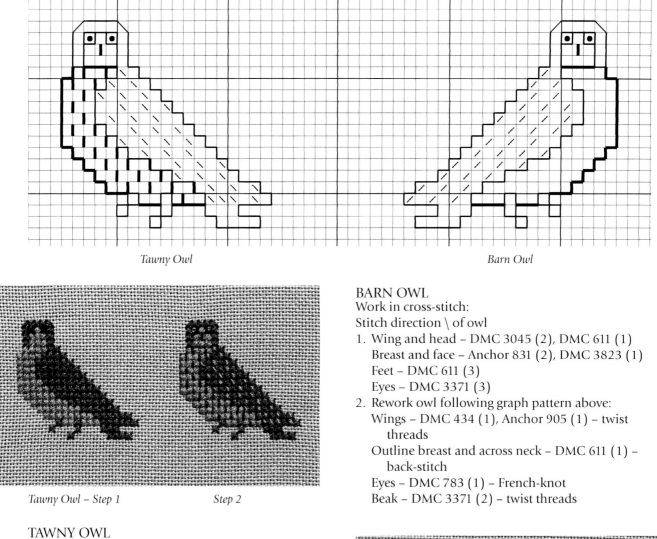

Tawny Owl   *Barn Owl*

Tawny Owl – Step 1   *Step 2*

TAWNY OWL
Work in cross-stitch:
Stitch direction / of owl

1. Wing and head – DMC 610 (2), DMC 434 (1)
   Breast and face – Anchor 392 (2), DMC 3045 (1)
   Feet – DMC 610 (3)
   Eyes – DMC 3371 (3)
2. Rework owl following graph pattern above:
   Wings – DMC 3045 (1)
   Breast – Anchor 905 (2)
   Outline breast and across neck – DMC 610 (1) – back-stitch
   Eyes – DMC 783 (1) – French-knot
   Beak – DMC 3371 (2) – twist threads

BARN OWL
Work in cross-stitch:
Stitch direction \ of owl

1. Wing and head – DMC 3045 (2), DMC 611 (1)
   Breast and face – Anchor 831 (2), DMC 3823 (1)
   Feet – DMC 611 (3)
   Eyes – DMC 3371 (3)
2. Rework owl following graph pattern above:
   Wings – DMC 434 (1), Anchor 905 (1) – twist threads
   Outline breast and across neck – DMC 611 (1) – back-stitch
   Eyes – DMC 783 (1) – French-knot
   Beak – DMC 3371 (2) – twist threads

Barn Owl – Step 1   *Step 2*

SQUIRREL
Work in cross-stitch:
Check direction of stitches

Body – DMC 435 (1), Anchor 373 (1),
   Anchor 884 (1)
Work A in / direction
Work B in \ direction
Tail – DMC 435 (1), DMC 611 (1), Anchor 884 (1)
Work A in \ direction
Work B in / direction
White on breast – Anchor 831 (2), DMC 3823 (1)
Outline white – DMC 435 (1) – back-stitch
Red berry – DMC 355 (2), DMC 632 (1)
Eye – DMC 3371 (3) – French-knot

Fir Branches

Quite often it is not possible to include a whole tree motif into an embroidery design, particularly if it needs to be on a large scale and there is only a limited space available. An excellent alternative is to use a leafy branch, as this is a very effective means for conveying the presence of a tree, whilst at the same time introducing a new sense of scale into the design. The type of patterns made by the foliage will obviously depend on the species of tree you are working from, and many early samplers feature an oak branch in a number of decorative styles. I thought that these branches of pine needles and fir cones would provide a perfect setting for the owls and squirrels, making them appear as though they are hiding in the trees.

    The pattern for the stitches is really easy to follow and only involves the use of back-stitch and French-knots. Firstly embroider the owls and squirrels in their positions on the graph and then back-stitch the outline of the branches.

BRANCHES
Work in long-stitch:
Stems – DMC 801 (1) The dots between the lines
   represent the length of the stitch

The pine needles are actually very quick to complete, but try to keep the threads untwisted, as they need to lay flat to get the full effect of the colour. Once you have positioned the first stitch in each group, just count the pattern round the edge of the needles and it will be quite easy to see where you are working. However, you do not need to follow the pattern absolutely, and you could place the pine-needles in a more random fashion, if you prefer to work more spontaneously.

Needles – DMC 500 (1), Anchor 216 (1) – keep
   threads untwisted
Cones – DMC 3371 (2), DMC 434 (1) – French-knot

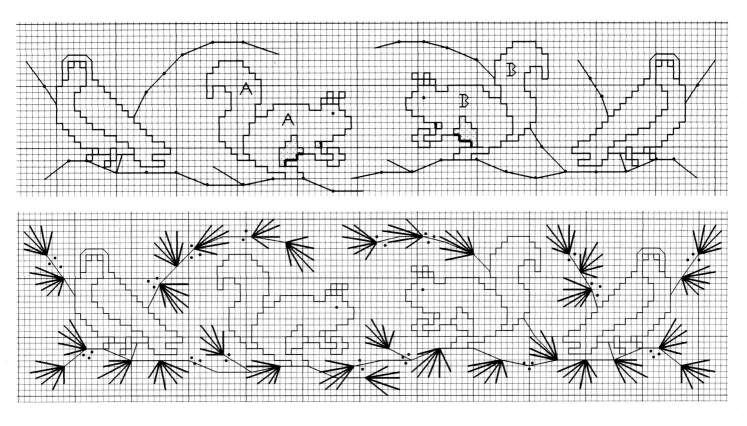

Hares

The variations in the flecked surface texture on the hare, give the motif a realistic appearance, and is another example of one of the many effects that can be achieved in cross-stitch, simply by combining three different shades of thread. The random pattern of the colours softens the rigid outlines of the form, helping to suggest the idea of the hares leaping about, and the use of a straight-stitch to depict the long pointed ears adds a delicate touch to the motif.

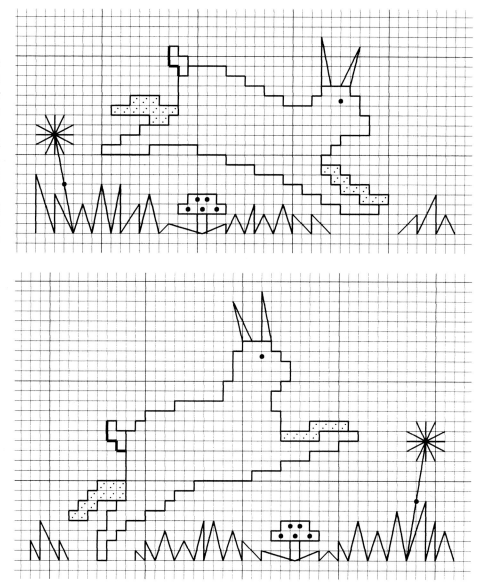

HARES
Work in cross-stitch:
Hares – DMC 610 (1), Anchor 373 (1), Anchor 831 (1)
Legs in shadow – DMC 610 (1), Anchor 373 (1), Anchor 905 (1)
Tail – Anchor 831 (2), DMC 3823 (1)
Tail outline – DMC 610 (1) – back-stitch
Ears outline – Anchor 905 (1) – long-stitch
Dark ear fill in – DMC 610 (1) – long-stitch
Light ear fill in – Anchor 373 (1) – long-stitch
Eyes – DMC 3371 (3) – French-knot

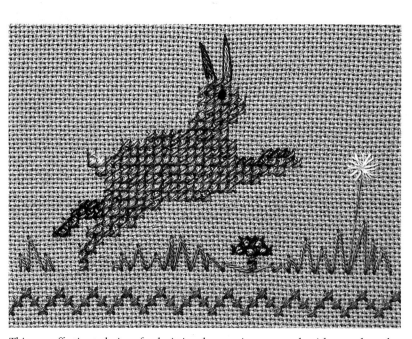

This very effective technique for depicting the grass is so easy and quick to work, and feels almost like drawing on the fabric. Also any number of little plants and flowers can be added at random and used to reflect the overall colour scheme in the design.

GRASS
Work in long-stitch:
Grass – Anchor 216 (1), DMC 3347 (1)

DANDELION CLOCK
Work in long-stitch:
Stem – Anchor 216 (1). The dot on the graph indicates the length of the stitches
Flower – DMC 3823 (1)

WILD MUSHROOM
Work in cross-stitch:
Red top – DMC 355 (1), Anchor 884 (1), Anchor 13 (1)
Stem – DMC 611 (3)
Spots – Anchor 831 (1), DMC 3823 (1) – French-knots

Winged Insects

Bees and dragonflies have always played an important part in my designs, and initially it was difficult to find a stitch that would best illustrate the delicate and fragile qualities of these little winged insects. I tried several different approaches, before discovering the technique that I call roll-stitch, which has proved to be the perfect answer. The body of the insect is formed by making a double straight-stitch, and then binding it with a series of small loops to create a coiled effect. The very structure of the stitch allows for two or more colours to form a striped pattern that closely resembles the markings on the insect's body. The final result looks so effective, and it is very easy to master the technique once you have practised it a couple of times; perhaps try it out on a spare corner of fabric before working on your design. However, if you make a mistake or are not satisfied with the outcome, just snip through the top threads and all the stitches will come away quite easily. For a diagram of roll-stitch *see* page 17.

Bees and Dragonflies

Body

1. Make a knot in the end of your thread and bring the needle up from the back of the fabric, just catching the weave of the cloth so that the thread does not pull through the hole.
2. Starting at the tail end of the insect, make a straight-stitch to the required length, and repeat the stitch in the same position, so that you have a double stitch.
3. Bring the needle back to the tail end and work a series of roll-stitches, being careful to keep the threads untwisted. If you hold each new loop in place with your thumb, it will stop the threads from slipping out of order. On a large dragonfly you will need about fifteen loops to cover the long base stitch, and on a bee you will only need to make about five or six loops.

Wings

These are made with a lazy-daisy stitch and, on the dragonflies, work a single straight-stitch up the centre of each wing, in another colour.

 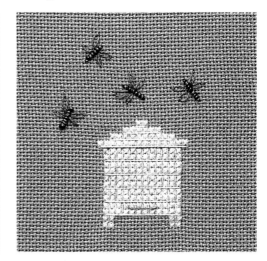

Dragonflies left to right: nos 1–4.

◆ I have marked the position of each insect on the large project graphs, but you need not follow these guide-lines exactly, and you are welcome to re-position, alter the scale or add more and different varieties as you wish.

1. DEMOISELLE AGRION
Body – DMC 825 (1), DMC 320 (1)
Wings – Anchor 872 (1)
Centre of wing – DMC 825 (1)

2. RED DAMSELFLY
Body – DMC 355 (1), DMC 400 (1)
Wings – DMC 415 (1)
Centre of wings – DMC 3823 (1)

3. EMPEROR DRAGONFLY
Body – DMC 501 (1), Anchor 168 (1)
Wings – DMC 3823 (1)
Centre of wings – DMC 415 (1)

4. GREEN LESTES
Body – DMC 320 (1), DMC 501 (1)
Wings – DMC 3823 (1)
Centre of wings – DMC 415 (1)

BEES
Body – DMC 3371 (1), DMC 783 (1)
Wings – DMC 646 (1)

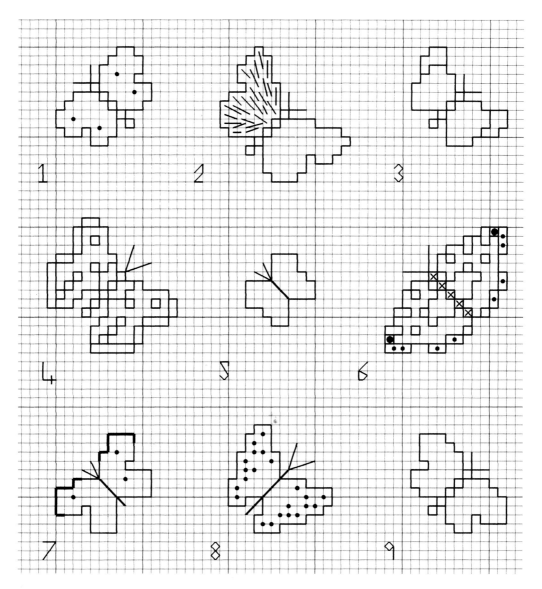

Butterflies

1. BRIMSTONE YELLOW
Work in cross-stitch:
Yellow wings – DMC 676 (1), DMC 725 (1), DMC
   612 (1)
Body – DMC 611 (2), DMC 612 (1)
Orange spots – DMC 920 (1), DMC 434 (1)
   – French-knot
Feelers – DMC 611 (1) – long-stitch

2. LARGE WHITE
Work in long-stitch:
Yellow outline – DMC 743 (1) –
   back-stitch
Body – DMC 783 (2), DMC 743 (1) –
   cross-stitch
White wings – DMC 3823 (1) –
   long-stitch
Feelers – DMC 783 (1)

3. ORANGE TIP
Work in cross-stitch:
White wings – DMC 3823 (1), DMC 612 (1),
   DMC 613 (1)
Orange tip – DMC 920 (1), DMC 434 (1)
Body – DMC 611 (2), Anchor 905 (1)
Feelers – Anchor 905 (1) – long-stitch

4. PURPLE EMPEROR
Work in cross-stitch:
Purple wings – DMC 333 (2), DMC 3721 (1)
Brown edges – DMC 611 (2), Anchor 905 (1)
White spots – DMC 613 (2), DMC 3823 (1)
Body – Anchor 905 (2), DMC 3371 (1)
Feelers – DMC 3371 (1) – long-stitch

5. CHALKHILL BLUE
Work in cross-stitch:
Blue wings – Anchor 920 (2), Anchor 392 (1)
Blue overstitch – Anchor 939 (1) –
   rework cross-stitch area with a half stitch
Body – DMC 610 (2) – long-stitch
Feelers – DMC 610 (1) – long-stitch

6. TORTOISESHELL

Work in cross-stitch:

Yellow wings – DMC 680 (1), DMC 725 (1),
    Anchor 884 (1)

Dark brown and body – Anchor 905 (2), DMC 3371
    (1)

Light brown centre – DMC 611 (2), Anchor 905 (1)

Blue spot on wings – Anchor 939 (2) – cross-stitch

Blue spots at edges – Anchor 939 (1) – French-knot

Feelers – Anchor 905 (1) – long-stitch

7. SMALL WHITE

Work in cross-stitch:

White wings – DMC 613 (1), Anchor 386 (1)

Body – DMC 611 (2) – long-stitch

Spots – DMC 611 (1), Anchor 904 (1) – French-
    knots

Outline wings – DMC 611 (1) – back-stitch

Feelers – Anchor 904 (1) – long-stitch

8. DUKE OF BURGUNDY

Work in cross-stitch:

Brown wings – Anchor 905 (2), DMC 3371 (1)

Red spots – DMC 920 (2) – French-knots

Body – DMC 3371 (2) – long-stitch, twist threads

Feelers – DMC 920 (1) – long-stitch

9. COMMON BLUE

Work in cross-stitch:

Blue wings – DMC 792 (1), Anchor 939 (1),
    Anchor 393 (1)

Body – Anchor 393 (2), Anchor 905 (1)

Feelers – Anchor 905 (1) – long-stitch

During the sixteenth and seventeenth centuries an enormous interest in flora and fauna was generated by the discovery of many exotic species in the New World. Publications, with detailed illustrations of birds and insects, provided a new source of inspiration for embroiderers, and this heightened interest soon spread right across Europe. Motifs of winged insects abounded, and the varying sizes and intricacy of the designs was probably the result of being copied directly from an engraving; with some interpretations portraying quite an accurate record of the subject, whereas other examples are obviously more imaginative and stylized in appearance. The most favoured approach was that of outlining the motif in back-stitch and filling in with a random satin-stitch, and I have used this technique to illustrate the Large White butterfly. However, you could just as easily work the motif in cross-stitch and then rework the area with a series of small straight-stitches, following the colours that are already there.

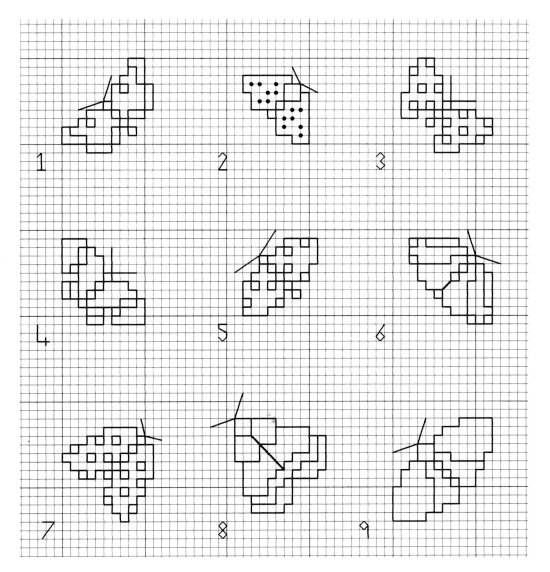

Moths

1. GOLD FRINGE
Work in cross-stitch:
Pink wings – DMC 316 (2), DMC 612 (1)
Yellow edges – DMC 725 (2), DMC 612 (1)
Yellow spots – DMC 725 (3)
Body – DMC 611 (2), Anchor 905 (1)
Feelers – DMC 611 (1) – long-stitch

2. WHITE ERMINE
Work in cross-stitch:
White wings – DMC 3823 (2), DMC 613 (1)
White head – DMC 3823 (3)
Body – Anchor 393 (2)
Brown spots – Anchor 905 (1) – French-knots
Feelers – Anchor 393 (1) – long-stitch

3. SPECKLED YELLOW
Work in cross-stitch:
Yellow wings – DMC 680 (1), DMC 725 (1),
    DMC 612 (1)
Brown spots – Anchor 905 (2), DMC 611 (1)
Body – Anchor 905 (1), DMC 680 (1), DMC 611
    (1)
Feelers – Anchor 905 (1) – long-stitch

4. PURPLE BARRED
Work in cross-stitch:
Brown wings – DMC 611 (2), DMC 612 (1)
Purple marks – DMC 355 (2), DMC 333 (1)
White marks – DMC 613 (3)
Body – Anchor 905 (2), DMC 611 (1)
Feelers – DMC 611 (1) – long-stitch

5. GREEN CARPET
Work in cross-stitch:
Light green wings – DMC 3347 (1), DMC 612 (1),
    Anchor 216 (1)
Dark green spots – DMC 500 (2), Anchor 216 (1)
Body – Anchor 393 (3)
Feelers – Anchor 393 (1) – long-stitch

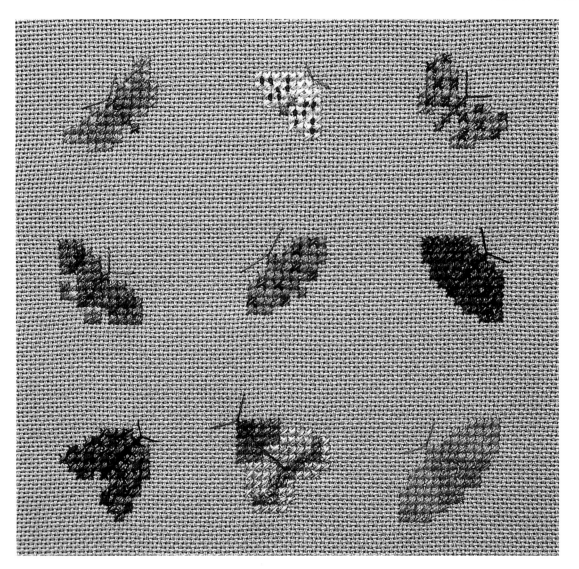

6. CINNABAR
Work in cross-stitch:
Red wings – DMC 920 (2), DMC 611 (1)
Brown marks – DMC 3371 (1), DMC 611 (1),
    Anchor 905 (1)
Body – DMC 3371 (3)
Feelers – DMC 3371 (1)

7. SIX- SPOTTED BURNET
Work in cross-stitch:
Brown wings – Anchor 393 (2), DMC 3371 (1)
Red spots – Anchor 13 (2), DMC 355 (1)
Body – DMC 3371 (3)
Feelers – DMC 3371 (1) – long-stitch

8. MOTTLED UMBER
Work in cross-stitch:
White wings – DMC 612 (1), DMC 613 (1),
    DMC 3823 (1)
Brown pattern – DMC 434 (1), DMC 611 (1),
    DMC 612 (1)
Dark brown head – Anchor 905 (2), DMC 434 (1)
Feelers – DMC 434 (1) – long-stitch
Line across back – Anchor 905 (1), DMC 434 (1) –
    twisted

9. GRASS EMERALD
Work in cross-stitch:
Light green wings – DMC 503 (2), DMC 612 (1)
Dark green wings – Anchor 216 (2), DMC 612 (1)
Body and head – DMC 503 (3)
Feelers – Anchor 216 (1) – long-stitch

There are actually many more species of moths than there are butterflies, but they are such elusive creatures that even the day-flying varieties are seldom seen. I was really surprised to find the range of colours and patterns that exists, and was equally intrigued by their fascinating names, such as Foxglove Pug, Magpie Moth, Scalloped Oak, The Forester, Ghost Moth and True Lover's Knot. I have chosen just a few notable examples to illustrate particularly the more colourful ones, although I personally love the soft brown earthy shades of varieties such as the Mottled Umber. The subject of moths was especially popular in early samplers, but by the nineteenth century the interest in detailed studies of insects had waned, and the motif was used more as a decorative way of filling in odd spaces. Despite the scale of these particular illustrations being quite small, I have used cross-stitch as the basic technique, as this allows me to mix the threads to create a more subtle and varied range of colours.

7 Water Mill

The imposing stone water mills that were such a common feature in eighteenth-century England, were probably thought of as too sombre and dreary to be considered as suitable subjects for an embroidery. These simple barn-like structures were certainly not as picturesque and appealing as the familiar windmill, with its characteristic pattern of paddles and sails. Small motifs of windmills were fairly popular in English embroideries throughout the nineteenth century, but not to the extent that they featured in European samplers. The significance and importance of these buildings was reflected in the endless variations, depicted in so many Dutch embroideries. This interest often extended to including stylized figures of the miller and his wife, and in one example, the workings of a horse-drawn mill are shown quite clearly with the farmer's wife in attendance.

I personally find the distinctive architecture of a mill building totally fascinating, and as an embroidery subject it has provided me with the opportunity to combine many interesting and unusual motifs and techniques. The mill makes the perfect setting for including an area of water, surrounded by reeds, dragonflies, wild ducks and a swan. Also, the border of delicate water-violets and row of trout, darting amongst the fronds of weed, further complement and enhance the overall theme.

OPPOSITE: The row of little figures in this composition suggests an ideal opportunity to feature your own family members. I have included some additional patterns of children playing or at school, and you could personalize the motifs further with you own colour schemes. The section of text could be replaced with any extra children, and names and dates arranged at the bottom of the design, extending and re-organizing borders where necessary.

Materials Guide

- *See* 'Preparing to Work', page 18.
- Zweigart fabrics are quoted for all projects.

FABRIC
Lugana 25 count Pewter
 Fabric size 19½ × 21in (50 × 54cm)
 Design size 11¼ × 12½in (29.5 × 32.5cm)
 Stitch count 143 × 164
Aida 14 count Summer Khaki
 Fabric size 18½ × 20in (47 × 51cm)
 Design size 10½ × 12in (27 × 31cm)
 Stitch count 143 × 164

THREADS
DMC and Anchor (+ denotes full skein):
Green – DMC 320 +, 500, 501, 502 +, 503
 Anchor 856 +
Brown – DMC 434 +, 611 +, 612 +, 801, 3031,
 3045 +, 3371 +, Anchor 373
Blue/mauve – DMC 926 +, 932 +, 825 +,
 Anchor 168 +, 872, 977 +, 978 +
Pink/red – DMC 355, 400, 407, 632, 3722,
 Anchor 884 +
White – DMC 613, 3823 +, Anchor 885 +
Black/grey – DMC 310, 317, 415
Yellow – DMC 676, 782, 783

- Mark in guide lines as described on page 19.
- Count up to narrow border above mill and begin with mill roof.
- The amounts of threads for each colour combination are indicated in brackets (*see* page 20).
- The alphabets for this design are nos 8 and 10 (*see* pages 121 and 122).

The Mill

The soft earth colouring of the mottled flint is created by combining three threads of varying tones, and working the building in cross-stitch. The three different shades of colour will naturally twist together as you work, to make an irregular, textured pattern that closely resembles the surface quality of the flint material. However, it may be necessary to occasionally give the threads an extra twist, so as to avoid any one area appearing too similar. The base colours for the water and swan are also worked in cross-stitch and the textural details are added later.

Detail of the mill and stream in the base colours.

◆ Following the graph pattern opposite and using the photograph above as a guide, work the whole area in cross-stitch, this includes the Mill building and arch, the water area and wooden bridge (*see small photo below left*).

MILL BUILDING
Flintwork – DMC 3045 (1), DMC 3031 (1), Anchor 885 (1)
Brickwork – DMC 434 (1), DMC 611 (1), Anchor 884 (1)
Window frames, granary door frame and main door – DMC 801 (2), DMC 3031 (1)
Granary doors – DMC 3371 (2)
Window panes – DMC 317 (3)
Roof – DMC 400 (1), DMC 632 (1), Anchor 856 (1)
Wooden Bridge – DMC 3371 (2)
Glazing bars – DMC 801 (1), DMC 3031 (1) – twist

WATER AND REEDS
Follow the water pattern on the graph opposite. Colours and stitch details are on pages 114 and 115.

◆ Re-work the details on the granary doors, main door and wooden bridge, using straight-stitch and back-stitch.

GRANARY DOORS
Using two sets of colours, re-work diagonal lines to form the three panels on the doors. Place the first colour as indicated on the graph right and rework the second colour between the stitches. Work the dark lines on the graph as one long straight-stitch.
First colour – DMC 611 (1)
Second colour – DMC 801 (1)
Dark lines – DMC 3371 (1)

MAIN DOOR
Work lines in DMC 3371 (1) – work as long stitches and double-stitch centre line.

WOODEN BRIDGE
Follow the guide-lines on the graph right and work three sets of horizontal long and short stitches, building up the colours to almost cover the base.
First colour – DMC 611 (1)
Second colour – DMC 434 (1)
Third colour – DMC 801 (1)

LETTERING
Back-stitch and cross-stitch:
Small lettering in back-stitch – DMC 801
The first letter of each word in cross-stitch is worked in a darker colour:
Letters T F F – DMC 611 (1), DMC 801 (1)
Other capitals – DMC 611 (1), DMC 434 (1)

BORDERS
Work narrow bands in cross-stitch:
Blue band – DMC 926 (1), Anchor 168 (1)
Blue spots – DMC 825 (2)
Green band – DMC 320 (1), Anchor 856 (1)
White spots – DMC 3823 (3)

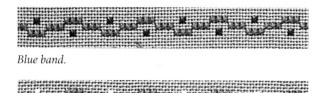

Blue band.

Green band.

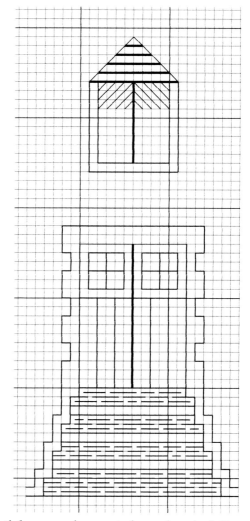

Graph for granary doors, main door and wooden bridge.

DRAGONFLIES
See details on page 95.

Fish

As an embroidery motif, the image of a fish has not on the whole generated much interest, which may well be due to the fact that the subject did not always fit very comfortably into the theme of the traditional sampler. Quite surprisingly, a number of early spot samplers include some very detailed examples of fish surrounded by simple water patterns, but it was not until the late twentieth century that the subject eventually gained some popularity as a cross-stitch design. I was really excited to find that this composition of the water mill, with its stream of gently undulating water, made an ideal setting for a row of leaping trout, playing in amongst the weeds.

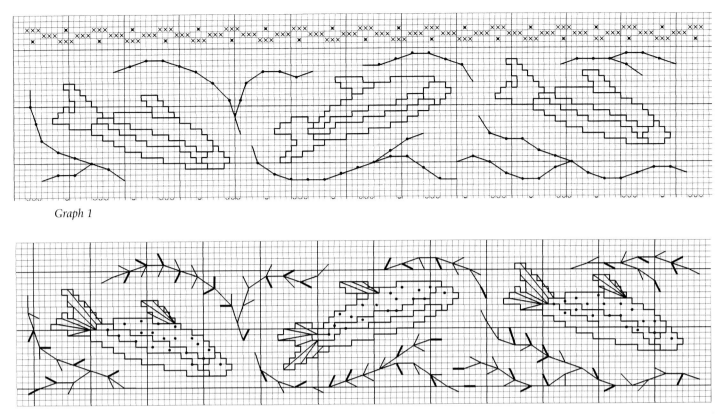

Graph 1

Graph 2

1. RAINBOW TROUT
Work the base colours in cross-stitch (Graph 1):
Green – DMC 503 (1), DMC 612 (1), DMC 415 (1)
Pink – DMC 407 (1), DMC 612 (1), DMC 415 (1)
Silver – DMC 415 (2), DMC 612 (1)
Head/tail/fin – DMC 612 (2), DMC 415 (1)

2. RAINBOW TROUT
Rework adding details (Graph 2). The spots are worked as French-knots, using four threads for the red spots and three threads for the brown spots.
Red spots – DMC 355 (2), DMC 611 (1),
   Anchor 884 (1)
Brown spots – DMC 611 (2), DMC 3031 (1)
Tail fins – DMC 611 (1) – straight-stitch
Eye – DMC 310 (2), DMC 3371 (2) – French-knot

1. WATER STARWORT
Work in back-stitch following the lines on Graph 1. The small dots indicate the length of each stitch.
Stems – Anchor 856 (1)

2. WATER STARWORT
Work the leaves in lazy-daisy, using two different greens. The light and dark lines on Graph 2 indicate the colour shade, but do not worry about being too precise, as long as you alternate the colours every so often.
Light lines – DMC 320 (1)
Dark lines – DMC 502 (1)

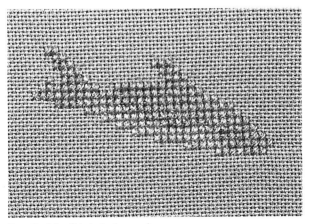

Detail of the fish in its base colours.

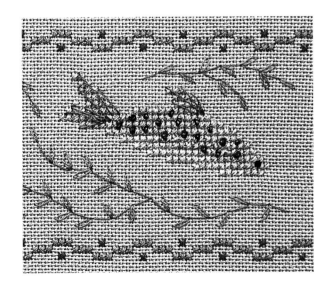

Borders and Wild Duck

This pretty little border of water-violets makes a delicate alternative to the more angular forms of the cross-stitch pattern. The motif is very easy to work, using only two basic techniques, including straight-stitches and the ever versatile lazy-daisy stitch. The subtle variations in the two-toned colours, on the leaves and flowers, and the way the light catches the different direction of the stitches, suggests a slight sense of movement, as though the plant was actually in the water.

WATER VIOLET BORDER
Stem – DMC 611 (1) – back-stitch. The dots on Graph 1 indicate the length of each stitch.
Leaves – DMC 502 (1), DMC 501 (1) – straight-stitch
Flowers – Anchor 884 (1), Anchor 872 (1) – lazy-daisy

MALLARD DUCK
Work in cross-stitch matching the symbols on the graph to the colours. The dark outlines on the graph indicate the back-stitch colours.

◆ – DMC 782 (2)
∵ – DMC 501 (2)
+ – Anchor 872 (1), Anchor 978 (1)
✕ – DMC 611 (1), DMC 434 (1)
‖ – DMC 611 (1), DMC 3031 (1)
c – DMC 613 (1), Anchor 885 (1)
z – DMC 611 (1), DMC 612 (1)
✚ – DMC 632 (2)
Outline/white – DMC 611 (1) – back-stitch
White lines/wings – Anchor 885 (1) – back-stitch
Collar – Anchor 885 (1) – double-stitch
Beak – DMC 783 (2) – double-stitch
Eye – DMC 783 (2) – French-knot

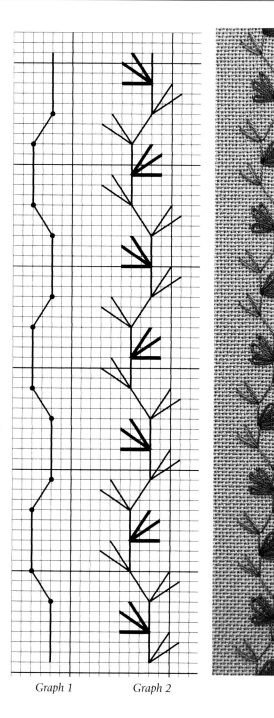

Graph 1   Graph 2

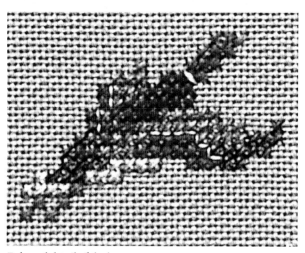

Enlarged detail of duck.

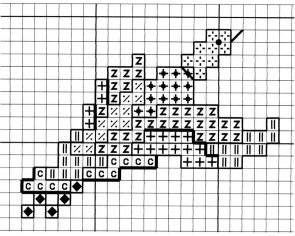

Match symbols on graph to colour codes listed above.

106

Figures

An interest and fascination with the costumed figure is evident throughout the history of embroidery. Some of the earliest samplers include beautifully worked motifs, revealing accurate details of contemporary dress. These little figures might appear quite unexpectedly in amongst the rows of patterns, as though they were also part of an exercise in recording and practising techniques and designs. Many of the early examples were depicted in more naturalistic poses, and were probably copied directly from an illustration, which was carefully sketched onto the fabric. The outlines were then picked out in running-stitch, which provided the base for building up the rich textural surfaces of the costumes. Much attention was focused on intricate details, and often beads and metallic threads were used to further embellish the garments and head-dresses, which represented the contemporary fashions.

However, alongside these elaborate textural interpretations, other examples demonstrate that cross-stitch was also a very popular choice of technique, and usually petit point was employed in order to accomplish the necessary details on the figures. Sometimes both approaches to the subject would appear in the same embroidery, with an equal concern for displaying and describing the current fashions of the day. During the eighteenth century, groups of figures representing family members were very common, often including several children and, on rare occasions, even household staff. However, the amount of personal attachment actually involved is not always clear, and probably many of the figures that appear in the schoolroom samplers were just motifs that went to make up the overall design. A very popular subject that appears in many samplers features a shepherd and shepherdess attending a flock of sheep, each dressed in period costume and holding a crook.

Figures are always a bit tricky to embroider, and it is difficult to create a form that gives a fairly realistic representation of a person, without it giving the impression of being a caricature. The actual weave of the cloth and relative scale of the stitches, in comparison to the amount of detail required to illustrate the faces, hair and hands of the figures, has always made this an area that poses certain drawbacks. Any number of techniques have been used in the past to overcome these problems, with each different method influencing the degree of detail possible. One solution, mainly employed in early examples, was to appliqué small pieces of silk or other fine fabric onto the embroidery, as these could be reworked with a finer set of stitches. In other cases, a similar technique might be used, only this time the faces and hands would be painted onto silk or paper, and then secured in place. The use of petit point was another obvious answer for faces and hands, as the tiny stitches helped to minimize any angular outlines, and I have sometimes combined this technique whilst still using an ordinary cross-stitch for the costumed area.

This detail of a family scene is from a larger commission, and shows the figures and animals worked in petit-point.

FATHER FIGURE
Work in cross-stitch:
Trousers – DMC 434 (1), DMC 611 (1)
Shoes – DMC 3031 (2)
Shirt base colour – Anchor 885 (1), DMC 3045 (1)
Shirt/chequer pattern – DMC 502 (1) – back-stitch
Hair – DMC 434 (1), DMC 3031 (1)
Hat – DMC 502 (1), DMC 611 (1), DMC 3031 (1)
Fishing rod – DMC 801 (1), DMC 3031 (1)
   – long-stitch
Fishing line – DMC 801 (1) – long-stitch
Hook – DMC 415 (2) – French-knot

BASKET
Work base colour in cross-stitch:
Basket – DMC 434 (1), DMC 3045 (1)
Handle – DMC 434 (1), DMC 3045 (1)
   – straight-stitch
Pattern – DMC 3045 (1) – straight-stitch

DETAILS
Face/hands/legs – DMC 407 (2)
Eyes – DMC 825 (1) – straight-stitch (double)
Mouth – DMC 355 (1) – straight-stitch

MOTHER FIGURE
Work in cross-stitch:
Shoes – DMC 434 (1), DMC 3031 (1)
Skirt chequered pattern:
   Dark squares – Anchor 872 (2)
   Light squares – DMC 3722 (1), Anchor 872 (1)
Lines across hem of skirt and on hat – Anchor 885
(1),   DMC 3045 (1) – long-stitch, twisted
Jacket – Anchor 978 (1), Anchor 977 (1),
   DMC 932 (1)
Blouse – Anchor 885 (1), DMC 3045 (1)
Hair – DMC 434 (1), DMC 611 (1)
Hat – Anchor 978 (1), Anchor 977 (1)

◆ The figures I have included in the projects are all
worked in cross-stitch, as the designs are easy to follow and can be used on any type of fabric. However, if you are working on an Evenweave fabric, you
could adapt the designs to use as petit point, should
you wish. Although a full cross-stitch poses certain
limitations on the overall appearance of the design,
much can be done to soften the edges through the
use of colour mixing. Flat, hard colours only serve
to re-enforce the geometric edges of the cross-stitch,
whereas with the use of subtle shades, created by
mixing and blending colours, the surfaces can be
broken up and the eye detracted from the outlines
of the motif. The use of the angled, half cross-stitch
is also very helpful when describing complex shapes
on a small scale. I have used this technique where I
feel it is absolutely necessary, although on the whole
I rather like the naïve quality of the figures, created
by the cross-stitch pattern.

GIRL
Work in cross-stitch – the length of stitches on the rope are indicated by angles on the graph:
Shoes – DMC 434 (1), DMC 3031 (1)
Socks and apron – Anchor 978 (1), Anchor 977 (1), DMC 932 (1)
Skirt – Anchor 872 (1), DMC 3722 (1)
Blouse – DMC 3045 (1), DMC 676 (1)
Apron – as for socks, with straps in straight-stitch
Hair – DMC 434 (1), DMC 611 (1)
Skipping-rope – DMC 434 (1), DMC 611 (1) – long-stitch

DETAILS
Face/hands/legs – DMC 407 (2) – cross-stitch
Eyes – DMC 825 (1) – small, straight-stitch
Mouth – DMC 355 (1) – small, straight-stitch

BOY
Work in cross-stitch:
Shoes – DMC 434 (1), DMC 3031 (1)
Trousers – DMC 611 (1), DMC 825 (1), Anchor 978 (1)
T-shirt/green – DMC 502 (2)
Shirt/red – DMC 355 (1), DMC 434 (1)
Hair – DMC 434 (1), DMC 3031 (1)

RAQUET
Work in straight-stitch:
Handle and outline – DMC 801 (1)
Strings – DMC 611 (1)

BALL
DMC 3045 (1) – straight-stitch – outline and fill in

These figures of small children have been planned on the same scale as the figures in the water mill project, and could either replace the original motifs or work alongside them.

Faces, Hands and Legs

The colours and stitches for the faces, hands, legs and features are the same for all the figures. I find it best to use small straight-stitches to depict the mouth and eyes, as they are easier to control and look less clumsy than a French-knot. Although the graphs indicate the position and size of the stitches, you may find that you need to make some adjustments and will need smaller stitches, particularly on the children's faces. Also, on some occasions the hands will need to be double-stitched to make them more obvious.

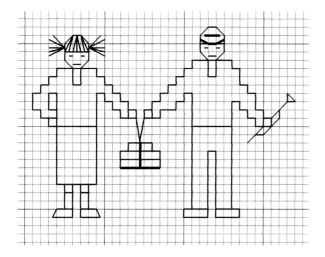

SCHOOL CHILDREN
Work both in cross-stitch:
Shoes – Anchor 905 (3)
Socks and shirts – DMC 613 (2), DMC 3823 (1)
Grey trousers/skirt – DMC 646 (3)
Red jumpers – DMC 355 (1), DMC 920 (1),
    DMC 611 (1)
Faces and hands – DMC 407 (3)

BOOKS
Work three in cross-stitch and one in straight-stitch:
Green – Anchor 216 (2)
Blue – Anchor 921 (2)
Brown – DMC 434 (2)
String – DMC 611 (1) straight-stitch

GIRL/HAIR
Work a cross-stitch base and over-stitch with five
straight-stitches to make a fringe – the pigtails are
worked in two colours:
Cross-stitch hair – DMC 611 (2)
Pigtails/first set – DMC 611 (1)
Fringe and second pigtails – DMC 680 (1)
Hair ribbons – DMC 355 (1) – straight-stitch

BOY/CAP
Work in cross-stitch and straight-stitch red bands:
Grey cap – DMC 646 (2)
Red bands – DMC 355 (1)

TRUMPET
DMC 680 (2) – straight-stitch

GIRL ON SWING
Work in cross-stitch:
Jersey/shoes – Anchor 921 (1), Anchor 939 (1),
    DMC 3810 (1)
Skirt – DMC 3721 (2), DMC 611 (1)
Socks – DMC 613 (2), DMC 3823 (1)
Hair – DMC 680 (1),
    DMC 434 (1), DMC 611 (1)
Swing/post and seat – DMC
    611 (2), DMC 612 (1)
Rope – DMC 611 (1) –
    straight-stitch

BOY RUNNING
Work in cross-stitch:
Shoes – Anchor 905 (2), DMC 434 (1)
Trousers – DMC 611 (1), DMC 612 (1), DMC 434 (1)
Jersey – DMC 502 (2), DMC 611 (1)
Hair – DMC 434 (2), DMC 611 (1)

GRASS AND BALL
Work in straight-stitch:
Dark green – Anchor 227 (1)
Light green – DMC 3347 (1)
Ball – DMC 611 (1)

FACES, HANDS, LEGS
DMC 407 (3)

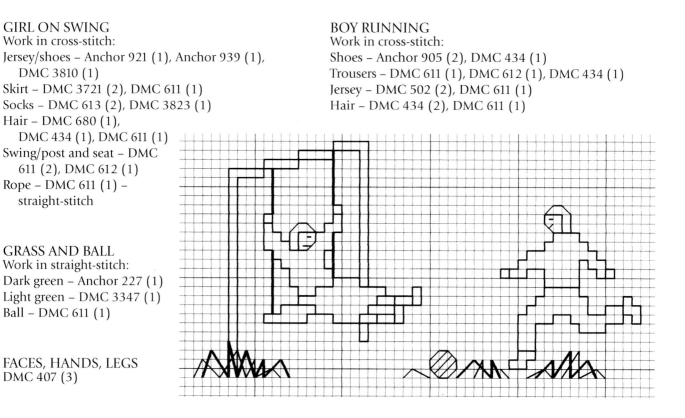

110

Water

Water is a wonderful element to translate through embroidery, as it is so suggestive of mood and atmosphere, and adds another dimension to the overall design, particularly as it gives one the opportunity to introduce the colour blue in all its varying shades and tones. I have included the subject of water in several pieces of work and each time I have tried to find a different method of depicting it; so as to capture the sensation of running and flowing waters, or that of a calm and tranquil surface. The combination of stitches and colours can be varied according to the type of water you are portraying, whether it be stream, river, lake or pond, and these variations in techniques also help to give the subject character and form.

Scenes including water as part of the overall composition were particularly popular with many of the embroidery schools in America during the eighteenth and nineteenth centuries. The busy trading ports situated around the large rivers would have had a great influence on the local communities in the area, and it is not surprising that this subject was portrayed so fre-

quently in the arts and crafts of that period. A variation on satin-stitch was the most common technique used to depict the reflective surface of the water, and was either worked as long horizontal stitches or as short vertical stitches arranged in rows; in a similar style to that which was often used to suggest an area of grass.

There are not so many references to this subject in English embroideries, and again it would depend very much on the inclinations of the particular schoolmistress as to the variety of patterns and subjects available in the classroom. The majority of examples I have come across are invariably worked in cross-stitch, and on some occasions only in rather dull shades of grey, which has rather a disappointing effect and does nothing to enhance that area of the embroidery.

The subject of the embroidery featured below was a family farm, set in the county of Norfolk, and I particularly wanted to capture the wild and solitary atmosphere of the narrow rivers of water that run through the fenlands. I have used a similar technique to the Petworth lake detail, only on this occasion I chose stronger and more contrasting colours, and laid the stitches in a more haphazard way so as create a sense of windswept water, rippling along as it travels.

Detail from an embroidery set in the Norfolk fens.

Still Water

This simple method for illustrating the subject of water is very easy to follow and looks most effective, as the layers of threads create a wonderful sheen that closely resembles the reflective quality of the surface. The dark base colour just shows through the covering of lighter stitches and gives added depth and interest to the final appearance of the water. I have used a range of subtle blues and greens in this example, to convey a sense of stillness and quiet, whereas more vibrant colours would suggest a very different mood.

When I began work on the sampler of Petworth House and grounds, which is featured below, I decided the water on the lake should reflect the grandeur of the building and convey a feeling of serenity and calm. I therefore worked a series of straight horizontal stitches over a dark cross-stitch base, using very soft silvery colours so that the water would not dominate the scene and detract from the other subjects: the swans and the statue.

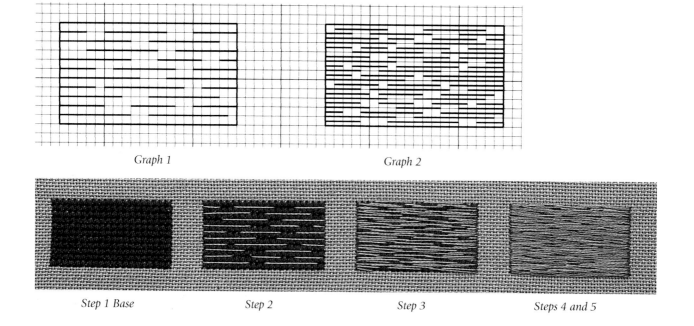

Graph 1   *Graph 2*

Step 1 Base   *Step 2*   *Step 3*   *Steps 4 and 5*

1. Work a dark base colour in cross-stitch – DMC 930 (3).
2. Using Graph 1 as a guide, rework the area in long-stitch – DMC 927 (1).
3. Continue with DMC 927 (Graph 2), working between the rows so as to build up the colour.

4. Then rework with DMC 932 (1).
5. Finally add two more colours, building up the surface, so as to almost cover the dark base colour: third colour – DMC 503 (1); fourth colour – DMC 926 (1)

Detail from a sampler of Petworth House and grounds.

Flowing Water

I feel that this very simple stylized design is ideally suited to suggest running waters, such as a stream gently flowing along its path. The wavy pattern combined with the lines of different colours in themselves give a sensation of water, and by adding a form of slanting-stitch to the surface, the notion of movement is further enhanced. The two colours that are used in the overstitching do not completely cover the base colours, and the combination of the three shades create a blend of softer tones that adds to the quality of the finished work.

I have used a width of five rows in this example of the water in the Water Mill project, but you can vary the amount of rows according to the design you are planning. Even as few as two rows of colour would be enough to convey the idea of water, and equally, a dozen rows of any number of colours would be just as successful. The slanting-stitch is worked diagonally across four cross-stitches and where the pattern steps down, the stitches need to be overlapped as you join the two rows together.

◆ The colours for each row are listed alphabetically and I have placed the three colours in each group together, under the relevant alphabet letter.

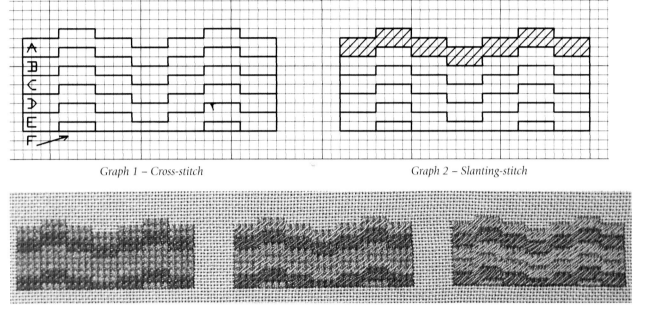

Graph 1 – Cross-stitch   *Graph 2 – Slanting-stitch*

Step 1 – Base   *Step 2 – First colour*   *Step 3 – Second colour*

◆ Work base colours in cross-stitch.
◆ Rework with slanting-stitch, placing the second set of stitches between the first set.

ROW A
Base – Anchor 977 (2)
First colour – DMC 932 (1)
Second colour – Anchor 168 (1)

ROW B
Base – DMC 825 (2)
First colour – Anchor 978 (1)
Second colour – Anchor 977 (1)

ROW C
Base– DMC 502 (2)
First colour – Anchor 168 (1)
Second colour – DMC 503 (1)

ROW D
Base – Anchor 168 (2)
First colour – DMC 932 (1)
Second colour – Anchor 977 (1)

ROW E
Work as colours in row B

ROW F
Work as colours in row C

This detail from a commissioned sampler shows the stream passing through a garden setting, with a row of flowering shrubs and a pretty little gate leading on to the bridge.

Dancing Water

I first thought of this fun pattern for depicting water when I was working on the sampler for Burton Pond, and I wanted to create the illusion of a dancing movement on the water's surface. As it is such a stylized design, the choice of colours need not be totally realistic and it provides an excellent opportunity to use a wide range of shades and tones to make an exciting and dynamic statement. I originally worked out the design through trial and error as I worked on the embroidery, with the result that most of the water 'shapes' are slightly irregular. Initially this worried me quite a bit, but on reflection I feel that the variations actually give the subject more character and individuality.

I have now devised a graph pattern for this design, making it is easy to follow the basic stages, and you can see from the examples that the waves are more uniform in size and shape. However, there is no need to be so precise and accurate when working the pattern yourself, unless it is an important consideration in your design. Rather than concentrating on making perfectly formed repetitive shapes, any small irregularities will make for a more expressive piece of needlework.

◆ Basically this design involves working a set of base colours in cross-stitch and then reworking the area with a satin-stitch, using the same colour. However, the technique is very open to interpretation and colours can be changed or added at random. I have used seven colours in this example, and have chosen to work with a different colour scheme to that in the Burton Pond sampler, but notice how the colours are much more intense once they are overstitched. If you decide to alter a colour midway, you can either change the shade of the second set of stitches, or ignore the base colours and re-work the area with a different colour scheme.

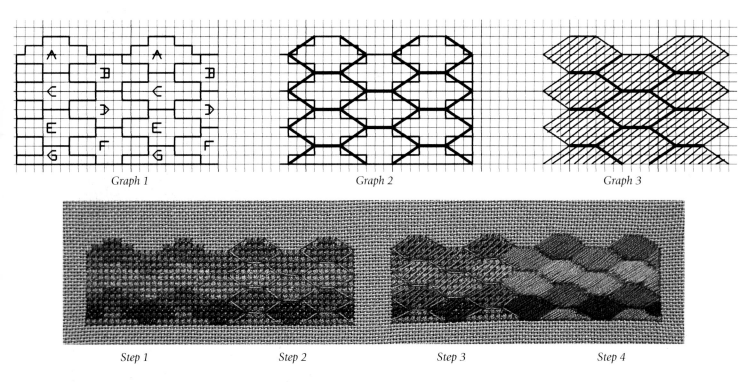

Graph 1   *Graph 2*   *Graph 3*

Step 1   *Step 2*   *Step 3*   *Step 4*

1. Work rows of the following colours across your design, in cross-stitch (Graph 1) and re-use the same set of colours to make the satin-stitches:
   A – DMC 931 (2)
   B – DMC 926 (2)
   C – DMC 503 (2)
   D – DMC 932 (2)
   E – Anchor 779 (2)
   F – DMC 924 (2)
   G – DMC 926 (2).
2. Following Graph 2, work a set of long-stitch lines over the cross-stitch area – DMC 926 (1).

3. Using the lines as a guide, fill in the shapes with a row of satin-stitches – work in one thread of the same colour as the base (Graph 3).
4. Continue with the same colours, placing the second set of stitches between the first, so as to build up the surface texture, and at the same time working over the long-stitch guide-lines, and covering them up.

◆ The guide lines in Step 2 are not absolutely necessary, and you may feel that you can judge the water shapes quite easily from the cross-stitch pattern.

Reeds

The suggestive forms of the wavering reeds and bulrushes not only make an effective edge to the water pattern, but also add a further dimension to the whole mood of the composition. The slight variance in the directions of the long-stitches, combined with the changing shades of the colours, creates a feeling of movement in the reeds, that contrasts perfectly with the formal construction of the building. It is so easy to add this motif to any area, especially as the actual technique is very simple to follow, and it could also be adapted to a smaller scale to represent grasses and sedges.

◆ Following the graphs below, work the reed outlines over the area of cross-stitch water, and re-work with straight stitches.

1. Outline the reeds and bulrushes in a long back-stitch – the dots indicate the length of the stitches:
   Reeds/outline – DMC 500 (1)
   Reeds/bent top – DMC 502 (1)
   Bulrush/stem – DMC 502 (1)
   Bulrush – DMC 801 (1)
2. Fill in the reeds with long-stitches, building up the surface with three layers of colour – fill in the bulrushes with French-knots:
   Tall reeds:
   First colour – DMC 500 (1)
   Second colour – DMC 501 (1)
   Third colour – Anchor 856 (1)
   Short reeds:
   First colour – Anchor 856 (1)
   Second colour – DMC 320 (1)
   Third colour – DMC 501 (1)
   Bent tops – DMC 320 (1)
   Bulrushes – DMC 801 (1), DMC 3371 (1)
      – French-knots

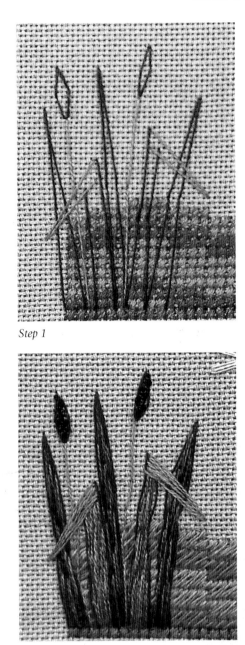

Step 1

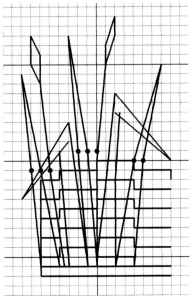

Enlarged detail

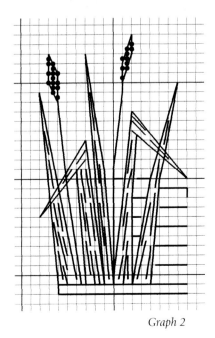

Graph 1

Graph 2

Swans

The sight of an elegant swan majestically gliding along the water, has been an inspiration to artists in every manner of visual and creative arts for generations. Some of the earliest recorded samplers include a number of spot motifs depicting the figure of a swan, or little scenes with the swan swimming above a pattern of water. The majority of English and American examples appear to be worked in more rounded, naturalistic forms, whereas some of the European motifs tend to be very angular and highly stylized. The distinctive silhouette of the swan makes such an interesting subject, despite its being all one colour, but it does seem a shame that in almost every example the swan is worked in plain cross-stitch. The large wing feathers of this magnificent bird combine to form a wonderful sculptural pattern, that is further complemented by the short silky feathers on the neck and body, and these contrasting surface textures make an ideal subject for interpretation through alternative stitch techniques.

A variety of motifs depicting all the wildlife in the area, was to be an important part of the composition for the Burton Pond sampler, and I decided to try and find a more exciting way of portraying the swans that have always nested there. Simply by using a long lazy-daisy stitch it was possible to create a surface texture that resembled the wing feathers, and in contrast I used a satin-stitch to help describe the smooth textures of the neck and body. I have included several swan motifs in various designs and each one is slightly different in style, as I do not usually work to a pattern. However, in order to illustrate the Water Mill project I needed to draw out a graph pattern, and I have described the various stages in detail, so as to make them easier to follow, although it is not essential to be quite so precise about keeping to the exact stitch plan, if you prefer a more random approach to your work. The main point, is to start with the top row of the long lazy-daisy stitches, and then work down, making slightly shorter stitches on each successive row.

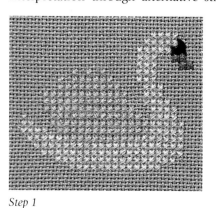

Step 1

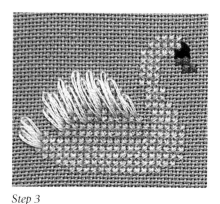

Step 2

Step 3

1. Work the base colours in cross-stitch – changing the direction of the top stitch (Graph 1):
   Neck and body – DMC 613 (1), DMC 3823 (1) – stitch direction /
   Wings – DMC 613 (2) – stitch direction \
2. Work the wings in long lazy-daisy, keeping the threads untwisted (Graph 2):
   First row – DMC 3823 (2)
3. Second row – DMC 3823 (2) – placing these stitches between the first set (Graph 3).

◆ As the following rows of lazy-daisy are worked, it may sometimes be difficult to locate the exact position of the needle in amongst the other stitches, but do not let it worry you. As long as the stitch is in the approximate position to that on the graph, any slight variations will add to the individual character of the motif.

Beak: work in cross-stitch, following stitch direction \
  Black – DMC 310 (2), DMC 3371 (1)
  Yellow – DMC 782 (2), DMC 783 (1)

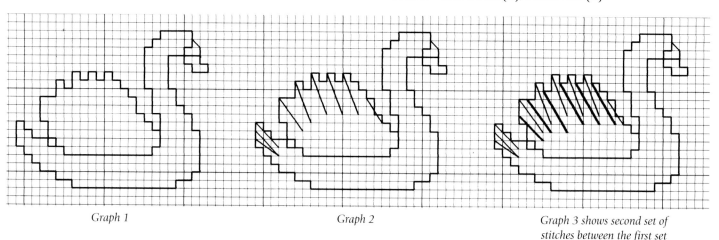

Graph 1   *Graph 2*   *Graph 3 shows second set of stitches between the first set*

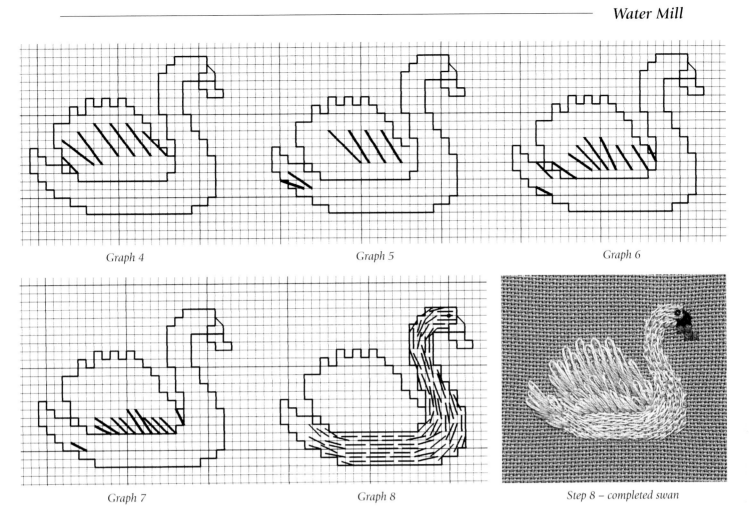

Graph 4   *Graph 5*   *Graph 6*

Graph 7   *Graph 8*   *Step 8 – completed swan*

4 and 5. Continue working in long lazy-daisy following Graphs 4 and 5:
Third and fourth rows – DMC 613 (2)

6 and 7. Continue in lazy-daisy using shorter stitches following Graphs 6 and 7:
Fifth and sixth rows – DMC 3823 (2)

8. Work in long-stitch following the guide to stitch positions in Graph 8:
Neck and body – DMC 3823 (1)

◆ These stitches only need to be the length of about two or three cross-stitches, and should be angled so as to follow the direction of the form.
Eye – DMC 310 (2), DMC 783 (1) – French-knot

A detail of the swans bobbing along on the water, from the Burton Pond sampler shown on page 7. The swan and water patterns were first worked in cross-stitch, and then re-worked with a series of stitches to emphasize the different textural qualities of the subjects.

8 Alphabets and Text

Sampler embroidery is one of the few mediums where various styles of lettering can be successfully used in both a decorative and informative way, as part of the overall design. The opportunity to record names, dates and actual places, and thereby personalize a pictorial image, is one of the main reasons for the popularity of this style of folk art. In general, the majority of early samplers were concentrated on the decorative pattern, but the use of text as part of an embroidery design became standard practice as young girls were instructed to sign and date their needlework exercises. The regular uniformity of cross-stitch was an ideal technique for interpreting the letter forms, and the teaching of alphabets and numerals could be conveniently combined in the one subject of needlework. Many pieces included long verses on a religious or moral theme, and often additional information such as the name of the school, teacher or building all helped to give an insight into the child's lifestyle of that period. However, embroidery was not only confined to the schoolroom, and was very much a part of women's everyday life, with love messages and even full-length letters being worked on fabric. Recording the family register was also a very popular subject, and in a number of samplers it became the central theme, with perhaps just a border of flowers arranged around the text or alternatively a tree design with the names and dates placed around the branches. Sometimes these samplers were kept unframed and added to by various members of the family, with each successive birth, death or marriage.

The renewed interest in sampler-making during the second half of the twentieth century, and the desire to commemorate personal events, has lead to the production of numerous kits and patterns for celebrating special occasions. It is amazing how quickly family circumstances can alter, as we live in a world of constant change, where property conversions and moving house are commonplace, combined with unlimited travel and the extended family. Information and details that were once familiar, may become vague and obscure within a few years, so any record of first names, surnames, place names and even locations will all become valuable pieces of family and social history.

Planning the arrangement and style of the lettering can be great fun and will add much interest to the finished work. I always look forward to this part of the embroidery, as letter forms are so satisfying to stitch and the rapid results are very rewarding. However, where you place the text in relation to the overall design, and the style of lettering that will best complement the theme of the work, will need careful consideration. First, write out all the details you wish to include on a piece of paper and perhaps try making a number of different arrangements with the words. Then count up the space that is available in the embroidery, choose an alphabet style that you feel is appropriate and chart out the letters on a sheet of graph paper, although at this stage you may have to make several adjustments to the spacing of the words and letters in order to get the text to fit neatly in the given area. There are many different styles of alphabets to choose from, and it is quite easy to alter the letter forms to suit a particular length by either extending or reducing the width of an individual letter, adding tails and flourishes, or placing the words closer or further apart. I have charted all the alphabets that occur in the designs, and you may notice that some of the letter forms have been very slightly altered once they are used in the projects. The colours you choose to illustrate the various pieces of text will also play an important part in the overall appearance of the embroidery, with light or dark tones placing a different emphasis on the words. I usually prefer to use fairly neutral colours for areas of cross-stitch text, although very small lettering in back-stitch may need to be worked in a deeper shade and, of course, decorative alphabets provide many more options for creating different effects. All the projects have an area of text included as part of the composition, and I have tried to suggest a variety of styles and arrangements, which could be interchanged with each other or further adapted to suit any number of occasions.

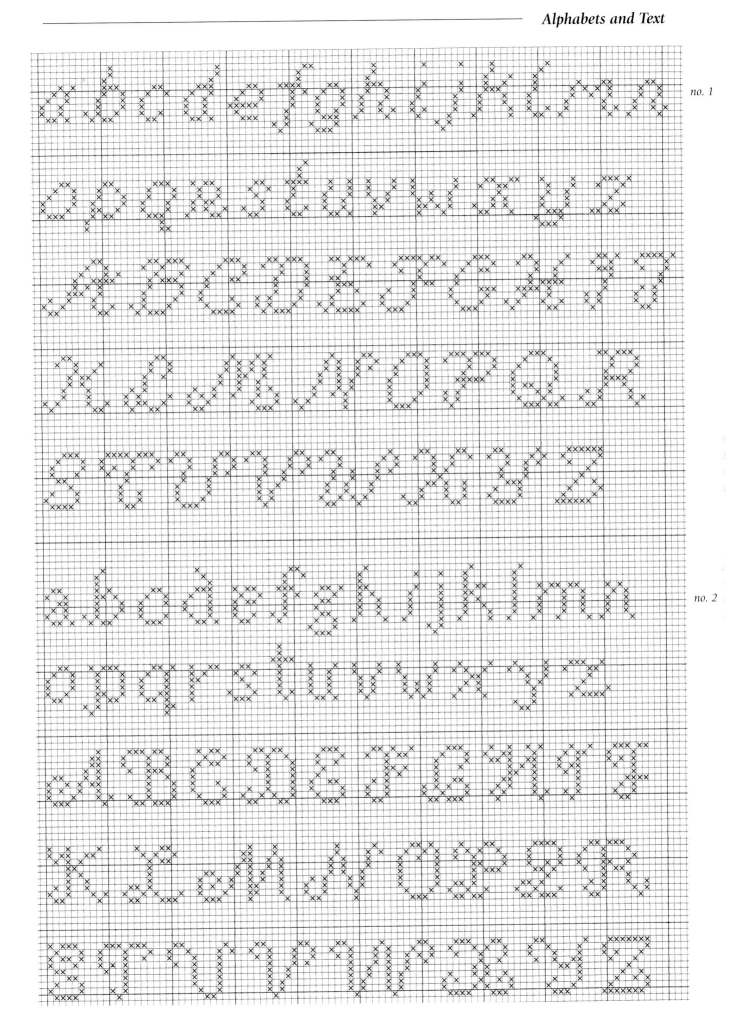

no. 1

no. 2

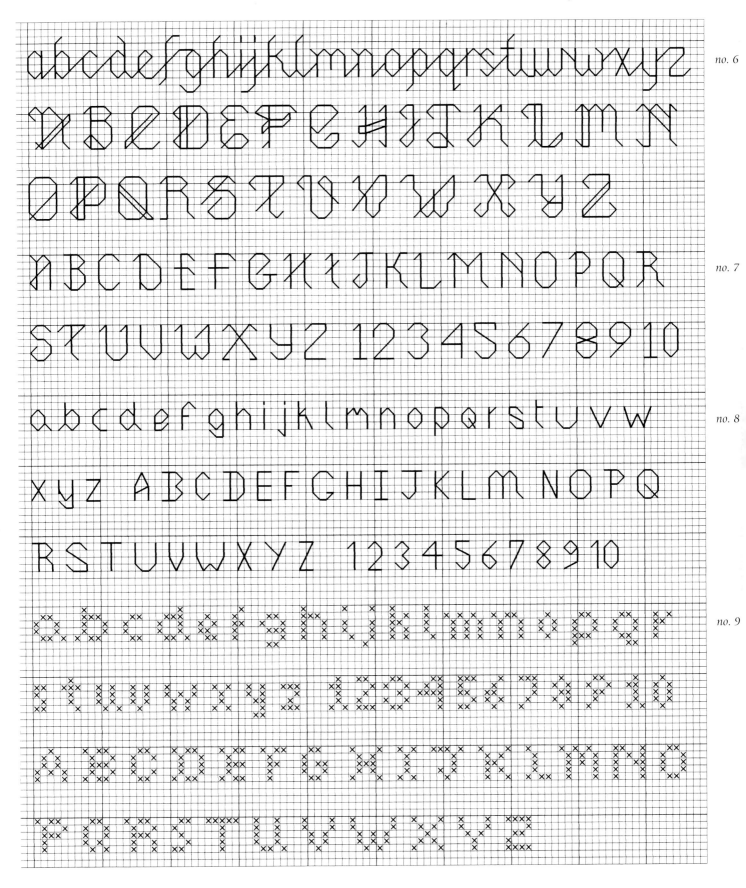

no. 6

no. 7

no. 8

no. 9

no. 10

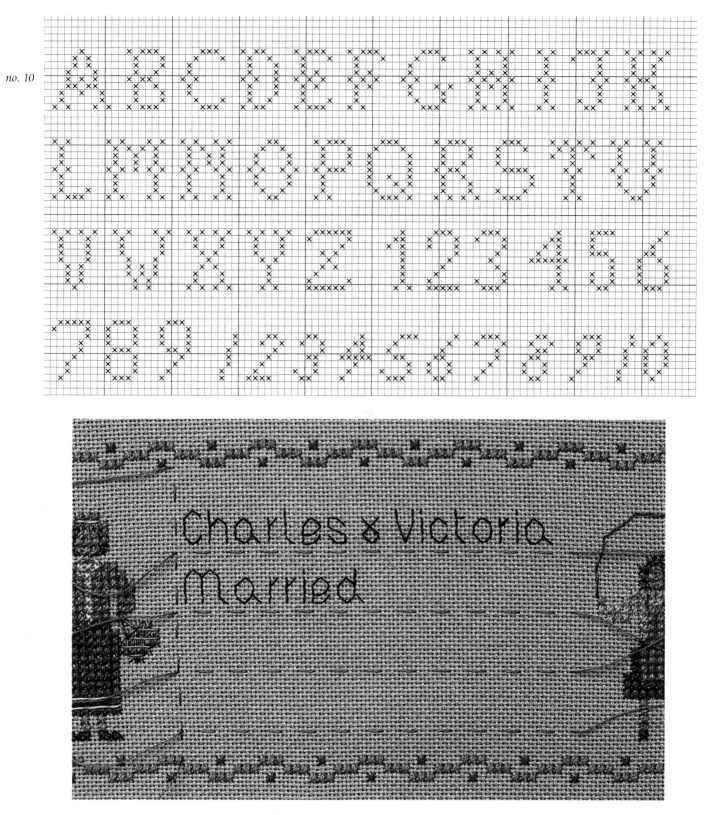

ABOVE: *Placing a piece of text in the centre of a design can sometimes be difficult to estimate accurately and I find it very helpful to mark out the area with rows of tram-lines. By working the tacking-stitches over and under each cross-stitch square it will be easy to match the graph pattern to the available space.*

OPPOSITE: *This very formal and decorative design would make an ideal choice for a row of alphabet letters in a sampler, or alternatively as a way of illuminating the first letters of particular words from a piece of longer text.*

List of projects and corresponding alphabet numbers:
1. Mothers Day
2. Country house
3. Farmyard animals
4. Woodland animals
5. Meadow Farm
6. Basket of fruit/hen house
7. Sunflowers
8. Water mill
9. Dovecote and rabbit
10. Water mill

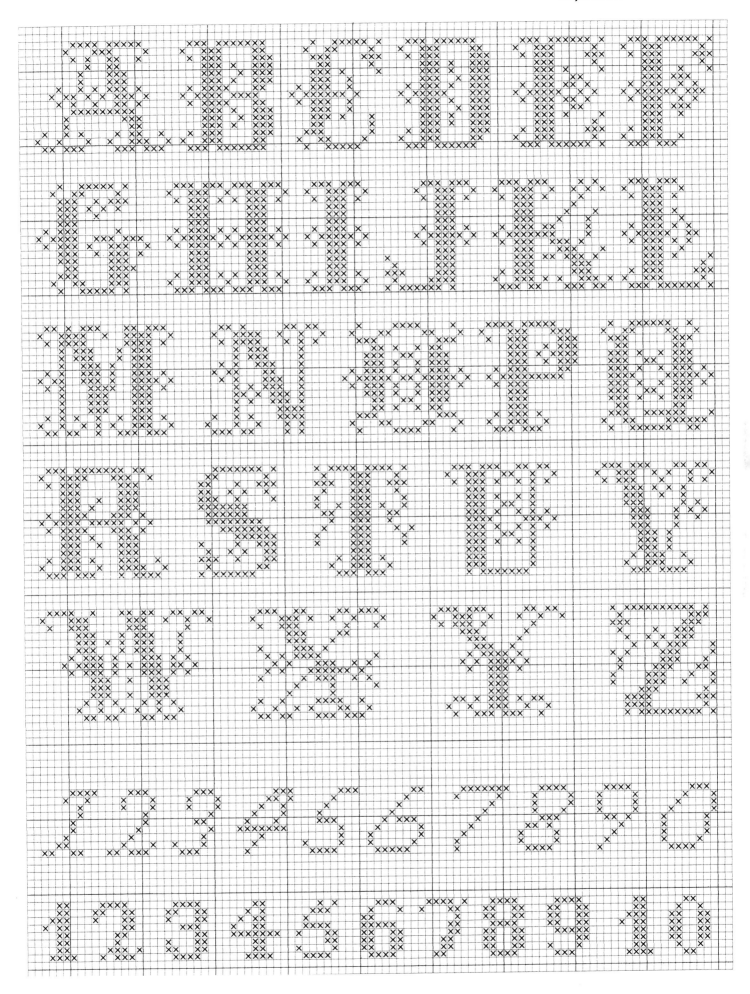

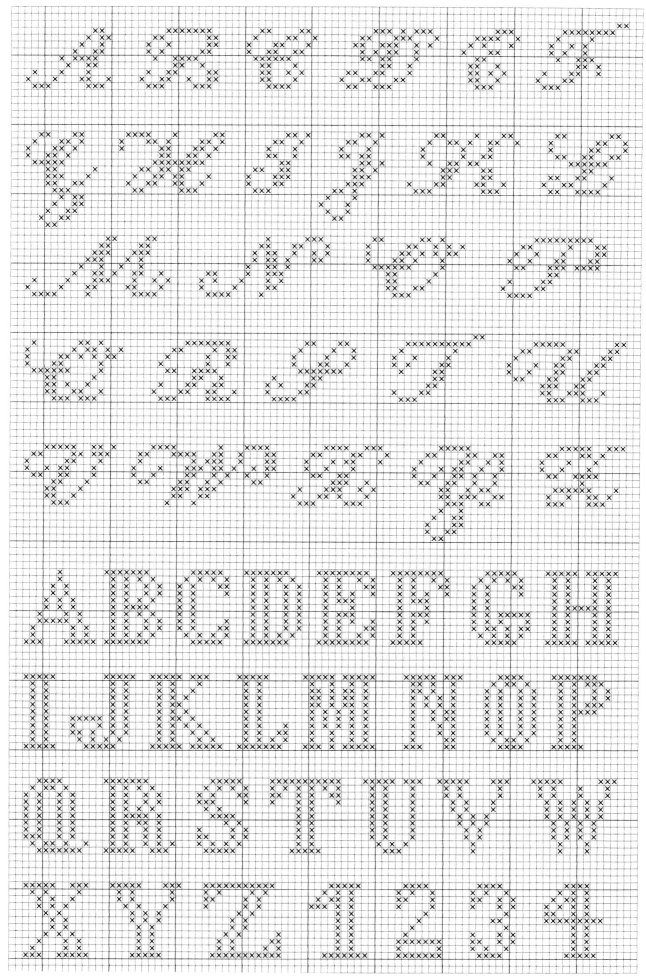

Additional alphabets.

Additional alphabets.

125

Bibliography

Browne, C. and Wearden, J., *Samplers from the Victoria and Albert Museum* (V&A Publications, 1999)
Colby, A., *Samplers* (Batsford, 1964)
Don, S., *Traditional Samplers* (David & Charles, 1986)
Fawdry, M. and Brown, D., *The Book of Samplers* (Lutterworth Press, 1980)
Gierl, I., *The Sampler Book* (A & C Black, 1987)
Jenkins, M., *House & Garden Samplers* (David & Charles, 1996)
Keyes, B., *Traditional Samplers* (David & Charles, 1998)
Krueger, G., *A Gallery of American Samplers, The Theodore H. Kapnek Collection* (Bonanza Books, 1984)
Lewis, F., *Needlepoint Samplers* (Studio Vista, 1981)
Mayor, S. and Fowle, D., *Samplers* (Studio Editions, 1990)
Meulenbelt-Nieuwburg, A., *Embroidery Motifs from Dutch Samplers* (Batsford, 1974)
Ring, B., *American Samplers and Pictorial Needlework, 1650-1850, Girlhood Embroidery, vols I & II* (Alfred A. Knopf Inc., 1993)
Sebba, A., *Samplers. Five Centuries of a Gentle Craft* (Thames and Hudson, 1979)

Useful Addresses

Museums with Sampler Collections

City of Bristol Museum and Art Gallery, Bristol, Tel. 01272 223571
Fitzwilliam Museum, Cambridge, Tel. 01223 332900
Hove Museum and Art Gallery, Hove, East Sussex, Tel. 01273 290200
The American Museum in Britain, Bath, Avon, Tel. 01225 460503
The Burrell Collection, Glasgow, Tel. 0141 649 7151
Wells Museum, Wells, Somerset, Tel. 01749 673477
Whitby Museum, Whitby, Yorkshire, Tel. 01947 602908
Victoria and Albert Museum, London, Tel. 0207 938 8500

Specialists in Antique Samplers and Needlework Books

Witney Antiques
96–100 Corn Street, Witney
Oxfordshire OX8 7BU
Tel: 01993 703902
Fax: 01993 779852

Marsha Van Valin, The Scarlet Letter
PO Box 397
Sullivan WI 53178 USA

Tel: 262-593-8470
Website: www.scarlet–letter.com

Ann Morgan-Hughes, Black Cat Books
Meadow Cottage High Road
Wortwell, Harleston IP20 0EN
Tel: 01986 788826
Website: www.blackcatbooks.co.uk

Main Suppliers

DMC Creative World Ltd
Pullman Road
Wigston
Leicestershire LE18 2DY
Tel: 0116 281 1040
DMC embroidery threads, Zweigart Aida and
Evenweave fabrics.

Coats Crafts UK
PO Box 22
The Lingfield Estate
McMullen Road
Darlington
County Durham DL1 1YQ
Tel: 01325 394394
Anchor embroidery threads, Kreinik metallic and
silk threads, Charles Craft Aida and Evenweave
fabrics.

Stockists

Campden Needlecraft
High Street
Chipping Campden
Gloucestershire GL55 6AG

C & H Fabrics, Brighton, Canterbury, Chichester,
Eastbourne, Winchester

David Morgan Ltd
26 The Hayes
Cardiff
South Glamorgan CF10 1UG

John Lewis Needlework Dept
Kingston on Thames, Aberdeen, Edinburgh

Peter Jones Needlework Dept
Sloane Square
London SW1 8EL

Sew Creative
97–99 King Street
Cambridge CB1 1LD

The Handicraft Shop
Queen Street
Exeter
Devon EX4 3SB

Voirrey Embroidery
Brimsgate Hall
Wirral
Cheshire L63 6JA

Cross-Stitch Drawing Package

Fulford Software Solutions
93 Penrhyn Crescent
Chilwell
Nottingham NG9 5PA
Tel: 0115 967 8761

Index